DON CHERRY'S
HOCKEY GREATS & MORE

DON CHERRY'S
HOCKEY GREATS & MORE

ANCHOR CANADA

Library and Archives Canada Cataloguing in Publication

Cherry, Don, 1934-, author
    Don Cherry's hockey greats and more. – Anchor Canada edition.

Previously published: Toronto: Doubleday Canada, 2018.
ISBN 978-0-385-69186-4 (softcover)

    1. Cherry, Don, 1934-. 2. Grapevine (Television program).
3. National Hockey League–Anecdotes. 4. Hockey players–Anecdotes.
5. Hockey–Anecdotes. 6. Sportscasters–Canada–Biography. 7. Hockey
coaches–Biography. I. Title. II. Title: Hockey greats and more.

GV848.5.C53A3 2019   796.962092   C2018-901234-X

Cover image: Bryn Gladding

Printed and bound in the United States of America

Published in Canada by Anchor Canada,
a division of Penguin Random House Canada Limited,
a Penguin Random House Company

www.penguinrandomhouse.ca

10 9 8 7 6 5 4 3 2 1

Penguin
Random House
ANCHOR CANADA

CONTENTS

DON CHERRY'S
HOCKEY GREATS & MORE

SCOTTY BOWMAN

Scotty Bowman trying to show me up by wearing
a tux on the *Grapevine* show.

THE WAR OF THE COACHES,
AND KNOWING WHEN IT'S TIME TO GO

SCOTTY BOWMAN IS THE WINNINGEST COACH of all time.
He has over 1,200 wins in the NHL, he's won nine Stanley
Cups as a coach and a total of 14 Stanley Cups as a coach
and executive. He's the only coach to win the Cup with
three different teams, and he won the Jack Adams Award
for NHL coach of the year twice.

Of course, I was coaching the Bruins and Scotty was
coaching the Canadiens when we met in the Stanley Cup
final in 1977 and '78. In 1977, we lost to them four games
straight. In '78, we lost in six games. We met again in the
'79 semifinals, and we were ready this time. Both teams

knew whoever won this series was a shoo-in to win the
Cup because they would meet the winner of the New York
Rangers–New York Islanders series. Neither the Bruins
nor Montreal had had a problem with either of those
teams in the regular season.

Just before the series, one of our defencemen, Mike
Milbury, who now does a great job on the NBC telecasts,
was asked what he thought about playing Montreal for the
third time in a row. Mike said, "Well, the first time we
played them in the finals, we were maybe a little happy
just to be in the finals and gave them too much respect.
The next year, we were a little more familiar with them
and now we knew this guy is a little bit of a backstabber
and this guy a little shy in the corner. Now, *this* time we
can't stand the SOBs."

After our morning skate in the Forum, Mike was on the
bench, looking up at all of the Canadiens' Stanley Cup
banners. One of the Montreal press corps asked Mike if he
was in awe of all the historical banners hanging from the
rafters. Mike said, "No, I was just thinking how chintzy
they looked."

That was our mentality during this series.

During that series, Scotty and I were going at it in the
newspaper. I remember saying, "I can't believe I'm getting
beaten by a guy who wears brown Wallabees with a blue
suit."

Before we taped the *Grapevine* show with Scotty, I was
wearing a really loud suit. Executive producer Ralph
Mellanby said maybe I should wear something a little
tamer. For the show, I wore a really sharp maroon jacket

with a great polka dot tie. When Scotty came out for the show, he was wearing a tux and a bow tie.

DON: Where are your brown Wallabees?

SCOTTY: Well, I'm the best-dressed coach now. No, those shoes were from Finland—they weren't those Hush Puppies.

DON: Remember the 1979 semifinals when I put too many men on the ice?

SCOTTY: Oh, yes, I think I remember. That was in the play-offs, wasn't it?

DON: No, seriously, did you see right off the bat there were too many? Truthfully, did you notice it?

SCOTTY: I was so excited I couldn't even count to six myself. One of the players yelled there were seven guys on the ice. So we started yelling at the linesman, and of course, I think it was John D'Amico called the penalty. I felt bad about it. But I was hoping we'd score, though, and I wanted to tie the game up.

DON: Sure, you felt sorry for, what, five seconds?

Like I said, Scotty and I were at war in the press. The day after the games, Scotty would call the press into his office and show videos of all the penalties (or what he thought were penalties) that the refs didn't call. Then the press came running over to me to tell me what Scotty said. I was saying the refs and NHL wanted a Montreal–New York final for TV ratings.

We went back and forth like that the entire series. The NHL was not too happy, but the press and the fans loved it. Back then, during the playoffs, *Hockey Night in Canada* broadcast the games and WSBK TV38 in Boston picked up the feed. I started saying that *Hockey Night in Canada* was biased and was pro-Montreal. I wasn't kidding. When Stan Jonathan and Pierre Bouchard went at it, they didn't show a replay. I knew that *Hockey Night in Canada* didn't show replays of fights, but I said the reason they didn't show that replay was because it was a Bruin beating up on a Canadien.

The Boston press and fans went nuts protesting *Hockey Night in Canada*'s treatment of the Bruins on their broadcast. A few games later, Mario Tremblay and Bobby Schmautz got into a fight and Mario cut Schmautzy. I left the bench in the middle of the game and ran into the control room where executive producer Ralph Mellanby was and said, "You didn't show a replay of the Jonathan fight—you better not show this one."

I think Ralph thought I was crazy.

I also noticed something else that seemed to have *Hockey Night in Canada* on Montreal's side.

> **DON:** In Montreal, you were always looking for an edge. I know for a fact that you went to *Hockey Night in Canada* when we were playing you and said,

"Look, when Guy Lafleur is tired and wants a rest, I'll adjust my tie and you go to commercial." Why is it that you want the edge over everybody?

SCOTTY: We had it figured out that every time we got a power play or a penalty situation, we wanted a rest. We didn't tell them when to call for a commercial. We just said, "When the other team gets a penalty, we'd like to get a rested power play." I guess the guy was a good hockey fan and maybe a Canadiens fan . . .

DON: You and I had a thing going in the papers that series. After the series, John Ziegler (the president of the NHL at the time) sent me a letter and it said, "Don, I want to congratulate you, the Bruins and the Montreal Canadiens on a stirring and unforgettable series. So it's with deep regret that I'm fining you $1,000." Did you get that letter?

SCOTTY: For us going back and forth in the press? Yes, I got one, but it was "Congratulations on a great series, I'm fining you $1,000."

After that series, both Scotty and I left our teams. I always joke that I was fired because of the penalty for too many men and stuff like that, but the truth is that Harry Sinden and the Bruins did offer me a contract. But if I took it, I'd have to be more like management—not be as friendly with the players and be less friendly with the press. I knew I couldn't agree to that. I think Harry knew that as well, and I said no.

So, after five years in Boston with four straight first-place finishes, two trips to the finals, two trips to the semi-finals and a winning percentage of .636, I left and went to Colorado. Scotty had been with Montreal for eight years, and with six first-place finishes, four Stanley Cups and a winning percentage of .661, he went to Buffalo.

DON: Four Stanley Cups and you leave Montreal. Why?

SCOTTY: Like anything else, I think it was time to move on. What it came down to was I was going to have to report to Irving Grundman. Irving and I never had a problem—he never bothered me and I never bothered him and I respected him as a businessman. I would have reported to Jean Béliveau. Jean Béliveau was a hockey man. He was not high-profile with the team at the time, but I couldn't get involved with someone who I didn't respect as a hockey man. Like I said, I respected him as a businessman. It was time to move on. You had already gone to Colorado; I wasn't going to have any more fun in Montreal, so time to go.

DON: Why didn't you go two years earlier? I would have had two Cup rings.

Scotty is right when he said it was time to go. Coaches, no matter how good they are or how much they win, know there is a time to leave. I feel a coach starts to lose it when he's with a club for five years. After that, I think the players start to tune him out. They know all his tricks, they've heard all the speeches, it starts to get a little tired. I had been with the Bruins for five years, I loved Boston and the players, but deep down I knew it was time to go, just like Scotty knew it was time to leave Montreal.

We taped this show in 1982, and it's hard to believe that Scotty went on to win four more Stanley Cups.

THE BLACK SWEATER AND CZECHOSLOVAKIA

I WAS AN ASSISTANT COACH TO Scotty in the 1976 Canada Cup. I've said it before and I'll say it again: this was the greatest team that was ever put together. We had six centres on the team: the Flyers' Bobby Clarke, the Kings' Marcel Dionne, Montreal's Peter Mahovlich, the Sabres' Gilbert Perreault, the Leafs' Darryl Sittler, and Phil Esposito, who was in New York. Just those centremen alone had combined for 614 points the year before. It was going to be hard for Scotty to keep everyone happy, and even though I interviewed Phil eight years after that series, he was still not happy.

> DON: All right, Phil, let's talk about '76. I think that was one of the best teams ever put together, but I got to ask, what was the deal with you and Scotty?

> PHIL: Well, at the time I didn't like Scotty Bowman and he didn't like me. I don't think he wanted me on the team, number one. I believe he was forced by either

you or Alan Eagleson to have me on the team because of what I'd done in '72, and I didn't want any part of that. I wanted to make it on my own laurels and I thought I did. Playing with Bobby Hull was a natural because I played with Bobby for three years in Chicago and we fit together. Mr. Bowman wanted Marcel Dionne, he wanted speed demons.

The next year, when I interviewed Scotty, I asked about Phil.

DON: Scotty and I coached in the '76 series, and when we were in Montreal, you told me that if you ever left Montreal, it would be on account of that organist.

SCOTTY: Yes, that was the time I got in trouble with Phil.

DON: Tell us what happened with Phil.

SCOTTY: It's a long story.

DON: It's the *Grapevine*, go ahead.

SCOTTY: We were playing the Russians in Toronto, and we all decided that we wanted a little more speed on the team. Unfortunately, the trainer, through some error during a morning skate, gave Phil a black sweater. Phil went up to you and asked what the deal was and you said, "Better ask Scotty."

DON: Yes, I can remember like yesterday, we were at the Toronto airport and Phil asked me what was going on. I told him, "Well, there's Scotty. Ask him." So Scotty comes walking down the hall and Phil goes up to him and gives it to Scotty pretty good.

Scotty and I had a laugh during the interview about that, but it wasn't funny at the time. Scotty and Phil went at it pretty good. Phil was upset because a black sweater made him a "Black Ace," which means you're not playing. The Black Aces started with Eddie Shore in Springfield. When you were in the doghouse or weren't playing, you practised in the black sweater. The reason it was black was that it hid the dirt better and Shore didn't have to wash it as often. I was one of Shore's Black Aces, and soon throughout hockey the black practice sweater was like a scarlet letter.

SCOTTY: There was Keith Allen, Don Cherry, Bobby Kromm, Al MacNeil, Sam Pollock, but if something went wrong, I was the guy that had to deal with it. The audience must know the famous goal that beat Czechoslovakia.

DON: I'm sure they [do,] but tell them again.

SCOTTY: Well, Don would come up to me before the game and say, "What do you want me to do tonight?" I'd say, "Go up to the box with Sam [Pollock] and keep Sam calm. If you got any messages, pass them down." We got into overtime against Czechoslovakia in the finals and Al MacNeil was with you and Bobby Kromm was with me, and we get a message from Don that Czechoslovakia's goalie, [Vladimír] Dzurilla, was really starting to come out. He was gambling. Don said, "If we get a chance, tell the guys to not just shoot, because they are not going to score. Just hold it and go wide." Darryl Sittler came down the ice and the Czechoslovakia players came running out at him, Darryl went wide, and as soon as he put it in, we all looked at Don from the bench and started waving.

DON: Go figure. Harry fired me in Boston two years later.

THE ST. LOUIS BLUES, AL SECORD AND COACHING STYLES

ALONG WITH ALL OF SCOTTY'S STANLEY CUPS, he won a Memorial Cup in 1958 with the Ottawa-Hull Junior Canadiens. Scotty then moved on to the Peterborough Petes, and then in 1967 the NHL expanded and Scotty went to St. Louis as the assistant coach of the Blues. The Blues got off to a slow start and their coach, Lynn Patrick, resigned and Scotty took over. Then the Blues took off and went right to the Stanley Cup final.

SCOTTY: I had my most fun in St. Louis. I remember one game, just before the seventh game of the Western Conference finals against Minny, and after the warm-up, Glenn ["Mr. Goalie"] Hall came to me — he used to do this all the time with me — and said, "Coach, you better keep an eye on me. I'm not moving very well tonight."

DON: Was it true he was always sick before a game?

SCOTTY: Yes, and that night I was sicker. I was 30 years old, it was my first year coaching and we're about to get ready to play the seventh game. I go to look for Doug Harvey. He's in the bathroom, having a shave about ten minutes before we go out for the game. I go up to Doug and say, "Doug, can I talk to you?" Doug says, "Sure, what's going on?" I went on to explain that Glenn said that he wasn't sure if I wanted him to play tonight. Jacques Plante hadn't played all playoffs. Doug looked at me and said, "Well, tell you what, Scotty, I'll keep both eyes on him, but tell him he's playing." So Glenn played that night and we went into two overtimes, and Glenn had 61 shots and let in one and Minny's Cesare Maniago had 55 and let in two. It was the best goaltending I can ever remember in the playoffs.

DON: You guys were against Boston in the finals [in 1970]. You knew Orr was going to score that overtime goal.

SCOTTY: If anybody was going to score, it was going to be Orr. I thought our team played pretty good that last game. We were up 3–2 and we got a penalty and

Johnny Bucyk tied it up. It was a great goal; you see pictures of it everywhere.

In case you're from the Moon, I'll explain to you that Scotty was talking about the famous photo of Bobby flying through the air after scoring the Stanley Cup–winning goal in the 1970 Stanley Cup final.

* * *

DON: Now, they say you're not close to the players, so what's this all about? You aren't close to the players?

SCOTTY: I don't think I'm that close. I couldn't coach the way you did. I couldn't coach that way. Especially when I got to Montreal. In St. Louis, it was a little different. We had older players, and like I said, I had my most fun in St. Louis.

Scotty and I had different coaching styles. He wasn't close to the players like I was. As I stated before, I was offered a contract after my fifth year in Boston, but Harry wanted me not to be so close to the players and be more part of management. I knew I couldn't do that, so I left.

Last year on Hockey Day in Canada, Ron MacLean interviewed Al Secord, who played for me as a rookie. Ron asked Al what I was like as a coach. He said, "I've seen Don speak the last five, 10 years, but I've never had a chance to talk to him, but I've always wanted to tell him — and maybe you can pass this along for me — he was the best coach I ever played for. Don was a player's coach; you wanted to go through the wall for him. He took care of his people and he was a pleasure to play for."

It was great to hear Al say that. Al was our first-round pick in the 1978 draft. He is from Espanola, Ontario, is tough as nails, and, in one rookie-camp game against the Flyers, Al had three fights. I knew he was going to make the team after that game. Al was not just a fighter. In his rookie year with us, he scored 16 goals. Al went on to have some great years. His best was when he was with the Chicago Blackhawks. His best seasons were 1981–82 and 1982–83. In those two seasons, Al scored 99 goals, had 450 minutes in penalties and got in 33 fights. Al would be making $8 million a season—or more—in today's NHL.

Al is also the answer to a pretty cool trivia question: Who was the last player to score 50 goals that didn't wear a helmet? Al Secord in 1982–83, when he scored 54 goals for the Hawks. Al wore a helmet his rookie year with me. To tell you the truth, Al didn't look very good wearing the helmet. So, about eight games into the season, we were playing the Leafs and the game was on *Hockey Night in Canada*. I told Al that if he took off his helmet, I would start him for the game and then put him on the first power play. How could a boy from Espanola turn down that offer?

Early in the game, the puck went behind the net and Al and a tough defenceman for the Leafs, Dave Hutchison, went at it. Al was a rookie and Dave was a five-year veteran from London, Ontario. Dave was six foot three and over 200 pounds. My heart went into my mouth. "What have I done?" I thought to myself. I never sent anybody over the boards to get into a fight, but if Al was starting to lose, I decided I was sending guys over. Al caught Dave with an uppercut and staggered him. To say I was relieved was an understatement. The two went at it again about three weeks later.

Today, Al's a pilot for United Airlines, so if you're ever on his flight, you better not act up or Al will come back and take care of you. Just kidding.

* * *

I am often asked what a player's coach is. It sounds like one that's easy on the players, lets them run wild and do what they want to do. It's the opposite. Yes, he trusts the players. He rarely has a curfew. The player's coach lives with the golden rule: treat your players like men. You treat the players like you want to be treated. Even though I never aspired to become a coach while I was a player, I'd often see a coach do something and think, "Geez, I'd never do that." It's funny, I really don't remember the good things a coach would do, but I always remember the bad things a coach did.

There is a philosophy in hockey that if a player becomes a coach, he has to change. I hear and read about it all the time. I don't believe that's true. To be a good player's coach, you have to get the players to respect you, but I'm sorry to say that they have to fear you too. You have to be fair and honest with the players, but if they break the rules, you have to be ruthless. But if you are a player's coach, you're closer with the players than you are with your general manager and owners. When I was fired my first year in Rochester I was told I was too close to the players. When I left Boston, I was too close to the players. When I was fired in Colorado, it was the same thing—I was too close to the players and not part of management.

I remember when Armand Pohan, who didn't know hockey, was in the office of his stepfather Arthur Imperatore (I have to say Arthur was a pretty good guy), the owner of the Rockies, and I knew my days were numbered with the Rockies.

Arthur asked Armand, "What do the players think of Don?"

Armand reluctantly said, "The players would walk on fire for him."

A few days later, Armand fired me for, as he said, not being more management-oriented. I have to say, he made me feel good for being honest in saying the players would walk on fire for me.

* * *

My players had fun and behaved. In all my years of coaching, I never suspended or fined a player. When I was coach and GM of the Rochester Americans, I told the players to stay out of a certain bar because that bar was trouble. Sure enough, I found out two of my leading scorers were at the bar, and the next morning I told them they were gone.

They said to me, "Grapes, we're your leading scorers. You can't get rid of us."

They were gone the next day, because eventually they were going to hurt the ship.

When I was in Boston, I couldn't do that because I was just the coach. When coaching in Boston, I didn't want anything getting out to Bruins general manager Harry Sinden. I'm betting he didn't want to hear about it either. If Harry heard about a player staying out too late or something like that, then he would have to take action. It was my ship, I was the captain, I would handle it. I always felt a team was like a crew on a ship. I remember I was in a fury about something and I said to the players, "The team is a ship, and if you do something to screw up the ship, I will drop you over the side of the ship in the night, never to be heard of again." It sounds drastic, but I meant every word.

Now, what happened if there was a good guy on the club that screwed up once or twice and hurt the ship? Well, he'd pay big time. I did not get rid of him, but he paid a heavy price. But I was always up front and honest with the players in what I expected of them, and the player knew it was coming and accepted his fate. I showed no mercy.

In Minnesota, Bobby Schmautz, one of my favourite players—but tough to handle as a coach—was out the night before a game. I was furious, but I didn't fine him because Harry would have found out, and I kept him in the lineup because, if I didn't, the press would be asking questions. But it didn't go unpunished. I knew Schmautzy wasn't feeling too good during the afternoon game, so I kept double- and triple-shifting him. He was throwing up on the bench, but he didn't quit or say uncle.

It was so bad that one of the other Bruins said, "Okay, Grapes, that's enough."

I threw him out there the next shift. I bet you he played about two-thirds of the game. We were tied 2–2 late in the third, and he had just come off a shift and almost collapsed on the bench. We had gotten a penalty and I said, "Schmautz, you're killing the penalty." He didn't say a word; just hopped back on the ice.

The faceoff was in our end. Minny won the draw and the puck went out to their point. Schmautz roared out to the point and blocked the shots. He was still on his feet and the puck bounced past the Minny defence. Schmautzy had a breakaway from our blue line. He roared in and snapped it top corner, scoring the shorthanded game-winning goal. He then collapsed in the corner.

When we got home that night, Rose asked me how Bobby was doing. I said, "Why, what did you hear?"

Rose said, "We saw him score and then fall down. The play-by-play announcer said he must have hurt himself blocking the shot because he just collapsed in the corner after he scored and the other Bruins had to help carry him off the ice."

See? Rose didn't even know.

I never understood suspending a player and, in the end, hurting the team. I made players pay the price in practice by skating them into the ground if they did something I didn't like. You suspended a player and it became all about that player and what he did, and that can be a distraction to the team. A classic example was back in the 2012 play-offs. Nashville was on a roll. They had just had their most successful regular season with 104 points. They went into the playoffs against the Red Wings and smoked them 4–1 and then went on to play the Coyotes.

Then they announced that they'd suspended Alexander Radulov and Andrei Kostitsyn for two games for breaking curfew.

They lost two out of the next three games and were out of the playoffs. After they announced the suspensions, it was all about those two players in the press. The team lost focus and it took three years till they won another round in the playoffs.

This is how I would have handled it: I would have kept giving it to them good in front of their teammates, calling them selfish and the whole deal. Then I would have skated them till they dropped, but they would not have been out of the lineup.

The one thing I learned over my career is that guilt is a great motivator.

* * *

A few years back, I couldn't believe how much stuff would come out of the Toronto Maple Leafs dressing room. Players would be talking to the press too much and "unnamed" sources were leaking things to the press on what was going on in the dressing room. When the new regime of Brendan Shanahan, Lou Lamoriello and Mike Babcock took over the Leafs, all that stopped. To me, the golden rule is that what happens in the dressing room stays in the dressing room. Deal with it internally, as they say.

As a player's coach, you should go the extra mile for players on your team and players who can help the team. In our 1978 training camp, we had a rookie defenceman named Mike Forbes. Mike was a six-foot-two, 200-pound defenceman who was drafted the year before. He came to camp but didn't have a contract. I liked the way Mike played. He was tough and we needed a little size on defence. Mike had a good training camp and had a few scraps. Harry wanted to send him down to Rochester, but I wanted to keep him up for a while to see what he could do.

One day, I told Mike he was going to play and he'd better do something. He played well that night, and after the game, I really praised him in the papers, saying he played a great game and all that kind of stuff. After that, Harry couldn't send him down. The other players knew what I was doing. Mike played about 30 games for us that season.

The same thing happened with Mike Milbury. In the 1976 training camp, he was our best defenceman and Harry wanted to send him down to Rochester, but I wanted to keep him. Even though we had big, tough forwards, our defence was not that big. In fact, I had to tell one of my best defencemen, Gary Doak, to stop hitting because he was always getting hurt when he took a run at the other teams' big wingers. I told him to stop hitting and that if didn't, he was being selfish. So I needed some defence with size.

Harry wanted to send Mike down and keep a first-round pick named Doug Halward. Doug was a smooth-skating defenceman, but that's not what I needed at the time.

When Doug came to camp, he was just getting over being sick and he wasn't ready to be in the NHL.

Harry and I went to war. The players knew I wanted to keep Milbury—as I said, he was the best defenceman in camp. If I didn't fight to keep him, the players would have known I was bowing to Harry's wishes. Harry put his foot down and Doug stayed, but he broke his leg less than 20 games into the season and Mike was called up.

He never looked back and played 12 years for the Bruins.

* * *

If my team got an injury, I would not call up a player from the minors. I didn't want him moping around, hurting the ship. If a player was injured, I just wanted to play short-handed. The players loved it. The guys on the fourth line would play a lot more. When a player is injured, there is always a fear that someone is going to come and take his job. On my teams, the players knew their jobs were safe when they were injured.

In the 1976–77 season, we had a ton of injuries. At one point, we had Bobby Schmautz, Gregg Sheppard, Gerry Cheevers, Stan Jonathan and Dwight Foster out of the lineup. I didn't want to call anybody up. Finally, we had to call someone up because the NHL told us it was a rule that you have to dress at least 17 skaters. So we called someone up from Rochester, and the guy played a few games and then Schmautz was ready to come back. The guy from Rochester scored two goals and was feeling pretty good. I had to tell him he was being sent back down. Remember, I didn't have any assistant coaches, so I told him myself. I wanted him to hear it from me. I've heard that at times some coaches get the trainers to tell the players they're going down, but I remember skating up to this guy in practice to let him know. I can still remember the look on his face. He wasn't too happy. I didn't want him hanging around, not dressing, not playing and being unhappy around the team, so he had to go back to Rochester.

Playing the third- and fourth-line guys a lot was the reason we set a record in the 1977–78 season with 11 skaters scoring 20 or more goals. Besides not calling up players from Rochester when the Bruins had injuries, as soon as we got up by three or four goals I would rest the first two lines and play the third- and fourth-line guys.

I never called the team or a player out in the press or embarrassed them on the bench.

Okay, two exceptions.

I called out Hardy Åström, my goalie in Colorado, more than a few times in the paper. The reason being I was trying to force my GM, Ray Miron, to get me a decent goalie. It backfired on me. The more I talked in the paper and told Miron to his face that we needed a goalie, the more he refused. I feel that Miron and I went to war about Hardy right off the bat. He had the owner's ear, and I was gone the next year.

Also, while in Colorado I grabbed defenceman Mike McEwen on the bench. We were playing Chicago and Mike was staying on too long. I kept warning him to keep his shifts short. We were up by a goal late in the game and he was on way too long and was gassed. He coughed up the puck in the corner, the Hawks snapped it home to tie the game and we ended up losing. When he came to the bench, I grabbed him by the sweater and told him how selfish he was.

Those are the two exceptions. The rest of the time, when I would give a player hell on the bench, I never got in his ear and made a big show of it. I learned you can give a hockey player all kinds of hell for doing something — just don't embarrass him in the press or in front of the crowd.

I remember poor Taylor Hall getting screamed at on the bench when he was with the Oilers. He was their leading scorer and was only a minus-4 for the season and was sent to sit at the end of the bench like a peewee player. I knew then that he was gone from Edmonton. Can you imagine how he'd look on the wing with Connor McDavid right now?

The other thing I would never do is give my team heck in the press when we were on a losing streak. I was tougher on the Bruins when we were on a winning streak than when we were on a losing streak.

Terry O'Reilly once said I was like the players' mother when we were losing. In my last year in Boston, we were on a pretty good roll. From mid-November to early January, we were smoking with a record of 20 wins, two losses and three ties. One day in the dressing room, I was telling the players to do something and I could see they were not giving me their full attention. I said I used to have a thing called Black Tuesday. Every Tuesday, I skated the team to death to keep them in shape and I was on them about our system of chipping the puck off the glass and chipping the puck deep into the other team's end.

I said to my goalie, Gerry Cheevers, "No one listens to the coach when you only lost two games in the last 25."

Gerry looked at me and said, "Sorry, what did you say?"

Then, in mid-January, the wheels came off. We won only six games out of the next 20. On January 28, 1979, the LA Kings walked into the Garden and beat us 5–3, and at that time we had lost seven out of our last nine games. The press was on us, and even some of the fans were booing. This is when you, as a coach, protect your team. The players would be looking to see if I would bail on them. When the press asked me about the losing streak after the game, I said, "We're on a long voyage and we've run into I don't know what. We've lost a few battles, but the war isn't over. The troops will be back. An awful lot of people are jumping off the bandwagon now. There'll be a few broken ankles before we're through, but they'll be back jumping on the band-wagon. We'll take all the flak and all the bull and regroup. Just wait and see."

The players were trying just as hard, and we were working every bit as hard as when we were on the winning streak. Sometimes teams get into a funk, and as a coach there is little you can do but support the players. When I see a coach dump on his team during a losing streak, I know exactly what he's doing, and so do his players. The coach is saying to the press, the fans and the owners, "Look, I'm doing my job; the players aren't doing theirs." In other words, "Don't blame me, blame the players."

Oh, yes, we did get out of that nosedive, but not until late March, when we lost only three out of our last 11 games.

Except for Hardy, I did the same thing in Colorado. It wasn't easy—we had some tough losing streaks in Denver. I had to say to myself, "I didn't bail on the Bruins; I can't bail on these guys." The players in Colorado tried just as hard as the Bruins players, but they weren't as good.

Just like you don't give up on your team, you don't give up on your key players. Towards the end of 1976–77, one of my top scorers was Bobby Schmautz. He was hurt a bit that season, but still managed 52 points in 57 games. But when he came back from his injury towards the end of the season, he couldn't score. He would miss open nets or ring it off the post. He was in a real funk. One day, Harry Sinden was in my office and Schmautz came in after practice and said, "Grapes, I'm playing terrible. Don't dress me." This was music to Harry's ears. He was not a big fan of Schmautzy. I told Bobby to get out; he was playing. My exact words were: "Get the ___ out of here." I knew the team would need him to get out of this funk to make a deep playoff run.

To get him out of the slump, I played him on his regular shift, every power play, and double-shifted him at times. I never understood how a coach could bench a player that was struggling. How do you expect him to get out of the slump sitting on the bench? There is a classic story of Ken Doraty. He didn't play one game and after that game the coach came in and started giving the players heck. Walked up to Ken and said, "Doraty, you can't score worth a damn." Ken replied, "Well, coach, it's tough to score from that angle at the end of the bench."

Bobby was struggling going into the playoffs. We were playing the LA Kings in the quarter-finals (we had a bye into the second round because we made first place; LA had beaten the Atlanta Flames 2–1 in the first round) and did Bobby ever break out of his slump. He scored a hat trick in the first game and potted two more in the second and ended up scoring 11 goals in 14 playoff games.

Another thing: I did *not* treat all the players the same. I know that goes against our Canadian socialist ways, but that's the best way to run a team. When I was in Colorado, we heard that the Leafs and Darryl Sittler were having problems, so we called to see if they would be interested in trading Darryl. They said we couldn't have Sittler, but we could have Lanny McDonald. So we agreed to trade Wilf Paiement and Pat Hickey for Lanny and defenceman Joel Quenneville. Wilf went on to set a Leafs record for most points by a right winger with 97, and that record stands today. As you know, Quenneville went on to be a great coach and win three Stanley Cups, and in 2000 he won coach of the year. I guess he learned a lot from me in Colorado—most importantly to GET A GOOD GOALIE!

Lanny really didn't want to come to Denver. The timing couldn't have been worse for him. He'd just bought a house in Toronto—a sure way to end up getting traded—and his wife, Ardell, was about to have their second baby. When Lanny came to Denver, I told him, "Look, just show up for the games and fly home on the days off." Ray Miron didn't like Lanny going home, but I said, "Too bad." Another nail in my coffin in Denver. He played 45 games for me and he got 45 points and 25 goals. I knew what kind of guy Lanny was and had no doubt he'd be ready to play when he hit the ice. Would I do that for every player I've coached? No, but for some of them I would.

You cannot treat Jean Ratelle the same way you'd treat a rookie. When I called an optional practice (which means just what it sounds like — you have the option to come to the practice or not), some players, like Ratelle and Brad Park, would not show up and some players, like rookies and other players, were expected to show up.

After one game with the Bruins, Rose and my daughter, Cindy, were in the wives' room (that's the room where all the wives hang out before and after the game), and one of the wives asked if it was an optional practice the next day. Another one of the wives, whose husband was expected to show up, said, "Well, it's optional for some."

So, driving home, Rose asked if it was an optional practice, and Cindy blurted out, "Well, it's optional for some." Now, I knew that didn't just come from Rose or Cindy. I asked who said that, but Rose and Cindy wouldn't crack under my questioning. But I knew who said it right away. I told Harry to get rid of the guy, and like most things I asked of Harry, he did. The toughest part was the player was one NHL game away from getting a full NHL pension. He went to the minors and never got a chance to play that last NHL game and missed his full pension by one game. I tried to get him when I was in Colorado so he could play that last game, but Ray Miron wouldn't go for it.

A player's coach is playing with fire. He's safe as long as he wins. If he gets on a losing streak, he has a good chance of being fired. You know why? Because he doesn't protect himself. A good example is this: his team loses, and the next day he knows his team needs a day off, that it would be good for the players, for the ship. So he doesn't call a practice. He is now leaving himself open for criticism from the GM, the owners and the press. The best thing for the coach to do to protect himself is to call a practice and grind the players into the ground. Then he's saying to everybody, "Look, I'm tough. Not my fault we lost."

I wanted to have an us-against-the-world mentality. You cannot lean to management when you're a player's coach, or you're looking for trouble. The reality is, if you are a coach, you are management, not a player.

I was my own worst enemy and I knew I was going to get it in the end. Don't all coaches? I love to tell the story that when you know you're being fired all the scouts, trainers and hangers-on stop talking to you. They figure if they are friendly with you and you're fired, they will be gone too. I don't blame them. How did I know my days were numbered in Boston? Every year for four years, I got a new equipment bag and it always had on the side: "Don Cherry, Boston Bruins, Coach." At the start of my last year, I got my equipment bag and it just said: "Coach." I knew something was up. I shouldn't make fun of coaches getting fired. As tough as it is on the coach, it's just as tough or tougher on the families.

This is not a lesson on how to become a successful coach in sports, even though I was coach of the year with my high school team, Pittsford High, and again in the AHL with Rochester, and in the NHL with the Bruins. If you want to be a coach today, you should try to find a happy medium between being a player's coach and a coach firmly on management's side.

I was a player's coach and Scotty wasn't. It's often said that the players didn't like Scotty. But they sure liked Scotty when they got their Stanley Cup bonus cheques.

PHIL ESPOSITO

Phil Esposito, one of the greatest goal scorers in NHL history.

BOBBY AND BRAD

I AM OFTEN ASKED WHAT THE greatest accomplishment of my hockey career was.

I always answer that the greatest accomplishment or feeling I had in hockey was that I—a career minor leaguer— had the greatest fortune to have Bobby Orr play for me.

As a coach, coaching Bobby was my greatest thrill. Before games, coaches always give a short speech, and when I was giving my speech to the Bruins, I would often say, "Remember, when Bobby has the puck, don't go offside." Bobby always thought I was joking, but I wasn't, and the other players knew it. You could say I was like the trainer for the legendary racehorse Secretariat. I guess the trainer could have helped Secretariat in some small way, but mostly you'd just get out of the horse's way and let him do his thing: being the greatest horse of all time. I guess you can say I felt the same way about Bobby.

It was beauty that he had his greatest year when I coached him. He had 46 goals, 89 assists, 135 points, a plus-123 and over 100 minutes in penalties. Bobby went on to win the Art Ross Trophy, and for the eighth and final time the Norris Trophy as the best defenceman in the NHL. Not to knock Brent Burns, who won the Norris in 2017, and deservedly so, but he had 29 goals and 76 points and was plus-19.

That year, 1974–75, Chicago and Tony Esposito knocked us out in the first round of the playoffs. After the last game in Boston, I was sitting by myself in my little coach's office in shock. Bobby came into the room—still in his equipment, sweat pouring off him. He sat down and said, "Grapes, I'm sorry. I didn't play well for you." I didn't know what to say. He didn't play well for me? Forty-six goals, 135 points, plus-123—and in the three playoff games, he scored six points.

I am also asked what my biggest regret in hockey was. It was that Brad Park and Bobby Orr didn't play together longer. We traded for Brad Park and Jean Ratelle in 1975, and Bobby and Brad played 10 games together. To me, they were the greatest defence pair ever in the NHL, even if it was just for 10 games. On the power play, they were deadly. Brad would feather the puck over to Bobby, who was a left-hand shot playing the right side, and he would blast it. Bobby would do the same thing for Brad, and he'd hammer it. In a game against the Minnesota North Stars, goalie Cesare Maniago said it was like facing two cannons on the point. Out of those 10 games they played, we lost only one—the first one they played together. Bobby had 18 points in that stretch, and Brad had at least 15. They were the first to play wide on the blue line while on the power play. They were a sight to behold.

The dream would end before a flight to Chicago. As I was getting on the plane, two players were carrying Bobby off of it. Bobby said, "My knee is locked." I got a call from Bobby the next day saying the doctor had operated on the knee. I knew he was out for the year.

I was very bitter and said, "What does that doctor do, carry a knife in his back pocket?" I guess I shouldn't have said that to a guy that just had an operation on his knee. Somehow I knew he wouldn't play for the Bruins again. The next year, he signed with Chicago.

There are many reasons I regret Bobby not playing longer for the Bruins. One is that I had a plan on how to protect him. I know Bobby is saying to himself as he reads this, "I didn't need anybody to protect me." Let me explain my plan. Bobby had over 100 minutes in penalties my first year in Boston, he had 40 fights in his career and was one of the toughest guys on the team. Terry O'Reilly and Wayne Cashman were the toughest on the team at that time. Soon after we also got Stan Jonathan, John Wensink and Al Secord. Teams used to mail points in when they played us. All these guys could play—scoring 20 goals or more—so they were not just mad dogs. We were the toughest team in hockey.

I would protect Bobby like I had protected Brad. Brad was leading the New York Rangers in major penalties when he came over in the trade. He had a few fights with us when he first came over. In a game against Detroit, he had a fight with a tough little guy named Dennis Polonich. I was livid. After the game, I had a meeting and told Brad: no more fighting. I explained to him that it was ridiculous to have my best player off for fighting. I did not want some jerk fighting Brad.

Brad was not happy. I talked to him about it at the All-Star Game in LA and he said, "What you told me was 'I don't want you fighting. In fact, I'm going to tell the league you can't fight. I forbid you from fighting and I'm going to tell the whole league.' Don, you can't do that. Do you know how many gloves are going to be in my face now that I can't fight? I'm going to take an awful beating out there. I won't fight, but don't tell everybody."

I said, "Brad, you don't understand. This is not the New York Rangers. If anybody touches you, we will take care of him. I guarantee you nobody will be whacking you in the face." Nobody did, because if you tried to bother Brad you paid dearly.

Brad only had to worry about the game and not about some jerk taking a run at him. From then on, he only had one fight per season. Brad was terrific for me. This is the plan I would have had for Bobby. I don't know if I could have stopped Bobby from fighting completely, but I would have tried. The word would have gotten out that if you touched Bobby, you would pay a heavy price. Just like the word got out not to touch Brad or Jean Ratelle. They thought Jean was finished in New York because of a bad back. He ended up leading the Bruins in scoring.

I also would have rested Bobby like I rested Jean Ratelle. I heard through the grapevine that the New York Rangers made their players practise every day. No days off. Like I said, Jean's back was bothering him when he came to us from New York. The Bruins would play Sunday nights, and usually our next game was on a Thursday. I told Jean, "I don't want to see you till Wednesday." He'd show up on Monday for practice and I'd give him heck, as much as you can give a guy like Jean Ratelle heck, and tell him to go home.

He was worried and said, "What if Harry [our GM] asks where I am?"

I said, "Don't worry about it. I'll just say you got the flu."

I think Jean didn't like the strategy at the start, but he did later in the season. I talked with Jean for Sportsnet at the All-Star Game in LA in 2017. We talked about him taking time off. Jean said, "It was great for me. That extra day sometimes at that age—36 or 37 years old—and you play hard every game, that extra day made a big difference."

I would have done the same for Bobby. I would have not seen him after the Sunday game till the Wednesday. It's a long year, and seasoned pros like Jean Ratelle and Bobby Orr don't need to be on the ice every day.

In an interview, they asked Jean about his time in Boston. He said, "If Bobby Orr hadn't been injured, we probably would have a Stanley Cup or two. Unfortunately, I played only 10 games with Bobby. I sat beside him in the dressing room and he assisted on my first goal with the Bruins. He's still the best ever as far as I'm concerned."

Yeah, we did pretty good without Bobby—four first-place finishes, 100 points every year—but I keep thinking of Brad and Bobby against Montreal. We were close to beating Montreal those last two years for the Stanley Cup. If we were close to beating Montreal without Bobby, what would we have done *with* him?

I think about those 10 games they played together. They had magic. Even *I* couldn't screw up these guys—just like Secretariat's trainer, just let them do their thing. But I look on the bright side of life. Bobby was seen at his best. That's how he should be remembered.

* * *

When I went to Boston, I was coming from the AHL to coach the greatest player ever in Bobby Orr and, at that time, the greatest goal scorer in the history of the NHL in Phil Esposito.

Phil was one of the first guests we had on the *Grapevine* show. When I was doing the cold opening, I said, "Ya know, Blue, I remember the first time I met the Boston Bruins and it was just before training camp. They were in a country club, they came in—they all had perms in their hair, lovely necklaces around their necks, they were all tanned up, they all looked like movie stars. I had to turn it into a team, and our guest tonight, Phil Esposito, helped turn those guys into a team."

When I sat down with Phil to do the interview he said, "I just heard you say in the opening that in your first year coaching us, that we were fat. What about you?"

I said, "Yeah, I was fat in the head." And I kinda was.

Looking back, I could see I was in a funny position when I became coach of the Bruins. It wasn't like the team was underachieving and Harry Sinden had fired the coach, wanting to blow up the team and start over. The reality was I was taking over a team that had been only two games away from winning the Stanley Cup.

Phil led the league that year with 145 points, including 68 goals. He came just short of breaking the NHL record of 152 points, with another record of 76 goals, which he had set two years earlier.

Bobby came in second in scoring; he had 32 goals, 90 assists and 122 points. In fact, the top four scorers were Bruins, with Ken Hodge scoring 50 goals and 105 points and Wayne Cashman racking up 89 points, including 30 goals.

Phil ended up winning the Hart Trophy and Art Ross Trophy; Bobby won the Norris Trophy, naturally. The captain, Johnny Bucyk, won the Lady Byng. The team had a record of 52 wins, 17 losses and nine ties, for a winning percentage of .724, best in the NHL. It led the league in goals with 349, and was third in the league in goals against. How many coaches take over a team that was two games away from winning the whole thing and was 35 games over .500?

You might think that this was a great team to take over, but the reality was if I didn't win the Cup, the season was a failure. No pressure.

Sometimes I wonder why Harry hired me. First, I think he liked the way I coached behind the bench. If you saw films of Harry behind the bench during the '72 Summit

Series, he was like a caged lion. He was constantly pacing back and forth. You could see the sweat stains coming through his jacket. He had fire coming out of his eyes. I coached like that in Rochester. It was all about winning. If someone had to die to win, well, too bad—that was our mentality. The second reason was I think Harry knew that, even though the Bruins were close to winning the Stanley Cup, he needed to make changes to the core of the team if they were going to keep close to Philly and Montreal. He was going to have to make changes, and he knew that I would agree with him once I started coaching the team.

There was no doubt Harry was taking a chance with me. I was a career minor leaguer with three years' coaching experience in the American Hockey League. I was successful. The Rochester Americans, of which I was coach and GM and which I built from scratch, had a winning percentage of .638, and I won AHL Coach of the Year.

One of the reasons for my success in Rochester was that the players related to me and I related to them. They were minor leaguers, and so was I. For 18 years I did what they were doing: ride the bus all day, play that night, get back on the bus, drive to the next city, stop off in the middle of the night at Howard Johnson's for dinner, get into the next city early in the morning, get up and go to a morning skate, have a steak for lunch, take a nap, then play the game and start it all over again. I was one of them, and the players on Rochester knew it.

* * *

Like I said, one of the first events I had with the Bruins was a pre–training camp dinner at a country club. When I arrived, the parking lot was full of Caddies and Mercedes. At the dinner, they were drinking $100 bottles of wine, along with steak and lobster. These were not my kind of guys. All the American Leaguers were hungry and just waiting to get a chance to make the NHL. These guys weren't hungry, to say the least. They were packing away the steak and lobster, though. I stayed for less than an hour, had one or two beers, had nothing to eat and then left.

Rose was surprised to see me home so early. When she asked if something was wrong, I said, "Rose, that's not what I want my team to be, drinking wine and eating surf and turf."

Rose got mad at me and said, "Why can't you enjoy yourself? You made the NHL. Start acting like it and not like an American Leaguer. This is just like the trip to Hawaii."

In the summer of 1973, Rose, Cindy, Tim and I had taken a family trip to Hawaii. I hated every minute of it. I worked in construction every summer for most of my life, and I hated being out in the sun. So during the day, I would stay in the hotel room while Cindy, Rose and Tim went to the beach.

Luckily for me, the Watergate hearings were on television, so I watched them all day. I am an expert on Watergate because I watched so much of it while I was in Hawaii. Tim started calling me a vampire because I only came out at night to have dinner with the family. The only thing I did during the day was visit the Pearl Harbor Memorial and a tour of the spot where Captain Cook was killed. Other than that, I was in the room, watching Watergate.

* * *

I said I was fat in the head when I first coached the Bruins because I didn't listen to my father's golden advice. He often said, "It's better to be shot for a wolf than a lamb."

When I coached Rochester I was a wolf, but my first year in Boston I was more like a lamb. Even though we were winning and were well over .500, the team was not playing great, except for Bobby who was tearing up the league. I kept saying to the players that we had to get going. They kept telling me, "Don't worry, Grapes, wait till the bell rings. We'll be there." Well, in the playoffs, the bell rang and we lost in the first round.

After the season, I met Harry in a Chinese restaurant. I said to Harry, "Look, Harry, I let you down. If you want, we can part ways and I'll go back to Rochester."

Harry said, "No way. There's no way we're winning with that team. We gotta change."

Harry told me he wanted the coach he saw in Rochester. I went back home to Rochester (I rented a small house in Saugus my first two years in Boston) and started painting my house. All summer long, I listened to the Who's "Won't Get Fooled Again" over and over. That was going to be my theme song. The next year, I wouldn't get fooled again. I was going to be like I was in Rochester. Harry was right when he said, "We gotta change." And boy, did he change things up. Three seasons later, there were only seven players left from my first year. Harry made the biggest trade in NHL history when he sent Phil Esposito and Carol Vadnais to New York for Brad Park and Jean Ratelle.

In those few short years, we went from a team that relied on a few players for scoring to a team that had eleven 20-goal scorers, and we went from the Big Bad Bruins to the Lunch Pail Gang, but we still drew 57 major penalties. The team started playing the way I wanted my team to play: covering the points, dumping the puck in, chipping it off the glass. I didn't want turnovers at their blue line, I didn't want shots coming from the point, and I didn't want players passing the puck up the middle. I wanted to cut down on mistakes as much as possible. Hockey is a game of mistakes, and most times the team that makes the least amount of mistakes wins.

* * *

So, you might ask what I didn't like about the way the Bruins played my first year. Three things really bugged me. First was how long the players' shifts were. I kept telling them I wanted short shifts. In Rochester, I was one of the first coaches that preached short, hard shifts. I liked my shifts to be about 60 seconds. Today, they go for 30 to 45 seconds; to me, that is too short. It's hard to get into the game in that short a time. In my first year in Boston, some of the shifts were over two minutes. Phil's shifts lasted forever. I swear, if the whistle didn't blow, Phil would have been on the ice the whole period. André Savard was the centreman who was up after Phil. Poor André would be straddling the boards, waiting for Phil to come off. Sometimes he would be straddling the boards for minutes on end. The players all joked that André was going to have trouble having kids when he got married from straddling the boards so much.

The second thing that bugged me was the attitude some of the veterans had. The team was called the Big Bad Bruins, and to me, they weren't. We did have some tough guys like Terry O'Reilly and Wayne Cashman, but overall the team was not that tough. When some of the Bruins were checked into the boards, they would turn around and slash the other guy, as if to say, "Hey, I am a Big Bad Bruin. You can't do that to me." We'd end up getting a penalty.

Now, some of the pseudo-experts of today will tell you that hooking is the worst penalty to take. They'll say that a player wasn't "moving his feet," and that's why he had to take the hooking penalty. Well, sometimes a player gets a step on you and you have to hook him so he won't get a good scoring chance. But slashing—that's just being stupid and selfish. I'd go nuts when we got a slashing penalty. I'd say on the bench, "Well, that really hurt him, didn't it? Way to go, you really showed him." I'd rather my players drop their gloves and get the extra penalty, or wait in the weeds and get him later, than take a stupid, nothing slashing penalty.

There was one other thing that really bugged me. I hated seeing the other team take shots at our stars. That was the biggest difference between my Rochester Americans and the Bruins my first year. Bobby Orr had three fights and over 100 minutes in penalties that season. I hated seeing Bobby fight. I seethed when players took a run at Bobby.

One game, someone took a cheap shot at him. I told one of the guys on the third line, "Don't let that guy get away with that." He took a few strides, then skated back to the bench and said, "Get away with what?" In Rochester, the players knew I didn't want anybody fooling with our stars. One game in Rochester, we were playing the Richmond Robins. One of our older veterans, Bob Ellett, who is the father of ex-Leaf Dave Ellett, got a roughing penalty. Back then, there was only one penalty box. The benches were on opposite sides of the rink, and the penalty box was next to the scorer's bench, which separated our bench and the penalty box. Now, Bob didn't fight much if at all. When they dropped the puck, I watched the game, but unbeknownst to me, the Richmond player in the box started to push and shove Bob. All of a sudden, John Wensink and Rod Graham left the bench, climbed over the scorer's box, jumped into the penalty box and went to town on Richmond. Of course, both benches emptied and it was a real humdinger.

That's the mentality I wanted on my team: don't fool around with our stars, or you'll pay the price.

It only took a few years to get that mentality on the Bruins. It started when John Wensink was called up from Rochester. It was the second-to-last game of the season. We needed to run the table those last two games to clinch first place. It was late in the first period in a tie game on Long Island. A good, tough little guy named Gerry Hart took a run at Jean Ratelle. The next shift, John went into the corner and had a great go with Hart. John got an extra two minutes. I don't think the players were too happy with John, but I jumped on the bench and hollered, "Way to go, John! Nobody fools with Ratty." Then I said to the penalty killers, "If you guys ever killed a penalty, make it this one." The penalty killers did their job, and late in the third, the game was tied at three. Guess who scored the winner on a backhand, top corner: Jean Ratelle. We ended up winning the game 5–3 and then whomped the Leafs 7–4 to make first place.

THE '72 SERIES

PHIL ESPOSITO DID MANY THINGS IN his hockey career. He set scoring records that took decades to break; he was a two-time Stanley Cup champion; he won the Hart Trophy in 1969 and 1974; he was the first player to score over 100 points in one season; he was a three-time Art Ross Trophy winner for leading the NHL in points; he led the NHL in goals for six straight years and was a First Team All-Star for six straight years.

Phil was the coach and general manager of the New York Rangers for three years and was the driving force behind getting a team in Tampa Bay. But to me, Phil's shining moment was the '72 Summit Series. They talk about great captains and great team leaders, but it's all nothing compared to what Phil did in that series. Not only did he rally the team, but he rallied the country.

> **DON:** I want to get to the '72 series. What was the mood in the training camp and before the first game?

PHIL: Well, we were told by scouts—the Toronto Maple Leafs' scouts, a team that ends up in last place all the time and we found out why—they told us they [the Russians] couldn't play very well, and their goalie, [Vladislav] Tretiak, couldn't stop a balloon. But what they didn't tell us was that the night they scouted him was the night after his wedding.

DON: Well, that does take something out of your legs.

PHIL: Yes, that's true. Then we started watching them practise and we realized these guys can skate, these guys can motor, these guys can handle the puck, these guys can do everything properly. We had to get into shape. A lot of the press and some of the fans were saying, "The Canadians were doing their training in the bar." I'm not saying we didn't have fun, because we did. We were told it was going to be a cakewalk. After that shock of losing the first game—

DON: You were up by two goals.

PHIL: —we just ran out of gas.

The first game between Team Canada and the Russians was on September 2, 1972, at the Forum in Montreal. Everybody thought it was going to be a cakewalk, as Phil said. It looked like that at the start of the game. Just 30 seconds into the first period, Phil scored. The crowd went nuts. About five minutes later, Paul Henderson scored and Team Canada was up two-zip. As Phil said, the team ran out of gas and the Russians scored four straight goals and didn't look back. They shocked not only Team Canada but the whole country with a 7–3 win.

I was in Rochester at the time, and I was listening to the game on the radio. Like the rest of Canada, I was in shock. When we lost, Rose started to tease me about Canada losing. I told Rose not to tease me about this — it was a big deal for me and a lot of Canadian hockey players.

Canada won the next game in Toronto with ease, 4–1. Phil had a goal and assist and Team Canada outshot the Russians 36–21, so everybody was wondering if the first game was a fluke.

The next game was in Winnipeg, and Phil got another goal and assist in a 4–4 tie. Again, Canada outshot the Russians 38–25 and really didn't play all that badly, but it was Phil that was keeping Team Canada close. This is when I think the fans and the press started to turn on Team Canada.

In the *Winnipeg Free Press*, they felt all was lost. "As a result of the tie, by the way, the situation now looks rather bleak for Team Canada. The best they can hope for is to take a 2 to 1 lead in games into Moscow and they are not sure about that by any means. Behind the Iron Curtain, their task will be even more difficult than it has been at home before a Canadian audience . . . the Kremlin bells are ringing now because the Soviet team will be stronger at home."

The fourth game was in Vancouver.

DON: Let me ask you about Vancouver. I played in Vancouver, and I told Rose if they ever get behind to watch that crowd. You did get behind, and they got on you.

PHIL: Well, it wasn't just Vancouver.

DON: That speech you gave after the game. I was watching on TV, and when you were done, I stood up and cheered.

The Vancouver game was on September 8, and the Russians got out to a two-goal lead in the first, then 4–1 after two periods, and it ended in a 5–3 fiasco. Once again, Canada outshot the Russians 41–31 and still lost. In fact, Canada had outshot the Russians in all four games, with a 147–107 advantage overall, but was down 1–2–1 heading to Moscow.

Just as I thought, the Vancouver crowd turned on Team Canada. They started booing the Canadians when they were down 2–0 after one period, and some fans started cheering for the Russians halfway through the game.

Things looked bleak. After the game, Phil was interviewed and he gave one of the greatest speeches in sports. Phil was out of breath and the sweat was just pouring off him. You could see that he was really down.

To the people across Canada, we tried, we gave it our best, and to the people that boo us, geez, I'm really—all of us guys are really disheartened and we're disillusioned, and we're disappointed at some of the people. We cannot believe the bad press we've got, the booing we've gotten in our own buildings. If the Russians boo their players like some of the Canadian fans—I'm not saying all of them, some of them booed us—then I'll come back and I'll apologize to each one of those Canadians. But I don't think they will. I'm really, really . . . I'm really disappointed. I am completely disappointed. I cannot believe it. Some of our guys are really, really down in the dumps. We know, we're trying like hell. I mean, we're doing the best we can, and they got a good team, and let's face facts. But it doesn't mean that we're not giving it our 150 percent, because we certainly are. . . . I mean, the more—every one of us guys, 35 guys that came out and played for Team Canada, we did it because we love our country, and not for any other reason, no other reason. They can throw the money, uh, for the pension fund out the window. They can throw anything they want out the window. We came because we love Canada. And even though we play in the United States, and we earn money in the United States, Canada is still our home, and that's the only reason we come. And I don't think it's fair that we should be booed.

That interview rallied Team Canada and the nation. Like I said, after that speech, I stood up and cheered.

Then it was off to Moscow.

DON: Tell us about Moscow.

PHIL: I don't ever want to go back. We were treated awful. We were not treated well at all. They treated us like animals, and the women that came over with us were treated even worse. They wouldn't let them eat with us and they were feeding them leftovers.

DON: Was it true that your rooms were bugged?

PHIL: Well, we were all looking for bugs, the little microphones, that we heard were in our rooms. Two of the guys found a lump in their carpet in the middle of their room. So they tore it back and there was a little metal box with five screws. So one of them had a pocketknife and unscrewed the box and opened it. There was another metal plate with four more screws. So they unscrewed that and then heard a loud crash. They had unscrewed the chandelier in the room below.

DON: What was it like playing over there?

PHIL: I thought the Swedes were the dirtiest players I ever played against for sticking you and spearing you. But the Russians! They did little things to you to try and get you off your game. It was like a mental war. I've said this before, and I got into a lot of trouble, but I tell the truth: I have often wondered how someone can kill another person in a war or anything—I never ever thought I could do it, but I am convinced in my mind and in my heart, to win that series, I would have killed.

In many ways Phil did kill the Russians. In an eight-game series, Phil scored seven goals and had 13 points, the most of any player on either team. There is no doubt in my mind it was Phil and Paul Henderson who rallied the team and made it possible for Team Canada to do the impossible: win the last three games in Moscow to win the series.

ESPO SCORES ON THE REBOUND AND TONY ESPOSITO

THE FANS IN BOSTON REALLY LOVED Phil, especially in North Boston, where there is a large Italian community. But in Boston, you're only as good as your last goal.

DON: What did you get that first year [1974–75]?

PHIL: I think I got 61 goals that year.

DON: And they said you had an off year.

PHIL: Yeah. I remember Leo Monahan [a sports reporter in Boston] wrote I slumped from '68. But you know, those things happen. Newspaper guys are going to talk like that for the rest of your lives.

DON: Well, they love me.

My first season in Boston, Phil had 61 goals and 127 points. When they talk in the media today about the great goal scorers in the history of the NHL, they rarely mention Phil. When the discussion comes up, of course they talk about Wayne Gretzky, Mario Lemieux, Brett Hull and the Rocket, Maurice Richard. But Phil paved the way for guys like Gretzky and Lemieux. Of course, the Rocket was the first player to score 50 goals in a season. Then Bobby Hull scored 54 and 58 goals to set the new single-season NHL goal-scoring record. Then Phil smashed that record by 18 goals two years later, when he potted 76. Phil scored more than 60 goals in a season four times before any other player had scored 60 in a season.

How did Phil score so many goals? Well, he wasn't a great skater, but he went right to the slot and nobody could move him. He was six foot one, 205 pounds, and when he went to the front of the net, you couldn't move him. As soon as the puck was on his stick, *bing*, it was in the net.

He told me, "Grapes, it's not how hard your shot is, or how accurate, it's how quick you shoot it. Never let the goalie get set."

The proof is in the pudding. Like I said, the fans in Boston just loved Phil, and I will always remember the sign they used to hang in the Garden almost every game. It read, "Jesus Saves, but Espo Scores on the Rebound."

DON: Okay, who was the toughest goalie to score on?

PHIL: Truthfully, I had a hard time scoring on Gump Worsley. I don't know, the little butterball covered a lot of the net or something. Well, of course it was my brother Tony—he was the best. You know, blood is thicker than water. To be honest, Don, you know, I had some good luck scoring against my brother.

We had Phil's younger brother Tony on the show shortly after we had Phil. So one of the first questions was:

DON: Who is the toughest guy to stop on a breakaway?

TONY: Well, in today's game, it would be Gretzky. He tries to outthink you. When I played, it would be a guy like Henri Richard—he was so fast and made some quick moves. Of course, my brother—he was so big and would wait for you to make the first move, so my brother was tough to stop not just on a breakaway, but anytime.

Tony was one of the great goalies in the history of the NHL. He broke into the NHL with the Montreal Canadiens but only played 13 games for them. The next season, 1969–70, was his rookie season with the Chicago Blackhawks, and he set a record for most shutouts by a rookie goalie, with 15. That record still stands today. Not only is it a record for the most shutouts by a rookie, but only one other goalie had more shutouts in a season, and that was George Hainsworth back in the late '20s.

In his rookie year with the Hawks, Tony had a record of 38–17–8, the most wins by a goalie that season. And he

had a 2.17 goals-against average to go with those 15 shutouts. He went on to win both the Calder Trophy as NHL
rookie of the year and the first of his three Vézina Trophies
as top goalie. He also was named to the First All-Star Team
and was runner-up for the Hart Trophy (MVP). That year,
Tony led the Hawks to the Stanley Cup final and took the
Montreal Canadiens to seven games before bowing out.

When Tony broke into the NHL, most goalies played a
"stand-up" style of goaltending, meaning exactly that—
they stood up and didn't go down to block shots. That was
because most goalies didn't wear a mask. Tony was the
godfather of the "butterfly" style, meaning that the goalie
drops down to his knees to make the save. Most goalies
today play a version of it; most use what they call a "hybrid"
butterfly style, whatever that means.

> **DON:** Why the butterfly? Everybody who watched you
> would ask why you were playing the butterfly style.

> **TONY:** The key to playing goal is always make the shooter
> make the first move; how you stop the puck doesn't
> matter. People seem to think because I went down
> on my knees like that, that I was out of position.
> That's not true; you're never out of position when
> you're on your knees. You got your faculties, your
> hands, and you can spring up immediately if you
> need to; to me, that's the most effective way to play
> goal. In fact, there is a guy playing [the interview was
> in 1984] today who was a First [Team] All-Star who
> played my style, Tommy Barrasso.

Like Tony, Tom Barrasso, who was playing for Buffalo at the time, was on the First All-Star Team, and won the Calder and the Vézina in his rookie year. I know Tony even helped Tom out during the 1984 Canada Cup.

Not only did Tony start the butterfly-style craze, but he also had a mask design that was ahead of its time. When Tony first played, the goalie mask was more of a fibreglass mask that fit tight to the face. As the years went on, goalies started to wear cages on helmets, and today the goalie mask is a hybrid of the old fibreglass mask and the cage. Later in Tony's career, his mask was an early form of the hybrid mask. He took a fibreglass mask and put a small section of cage across the eyeholes for extra protection.

DON: Now, tell us about your mask. You have the fibreglass and still have the bars. How did you come up with that?

TONY: In the old days, when I was young, there was no mask. Then came the masks, and that was a big step forward. Even though I had a mask, I kept getting hit in the eye because I had big eyeholes in my mask. I said, "Sooner or later, I'm not going to be seeing out of one of these eyes." Rather than change it to the full cage—which I think is very prohibitive, and stops your vision down below at your feet, and you lose the puck all the time, so I designed [it] to put these bars over my face mask, and it really helped me, and I think that's the direction it should go.

Tony was smart putting that cage over his eyes. The very thing that Tony was concerned about had happened to the Philadelphia Flyers' all-star goalie, Bernie Parent, in 1979. The Flyers were playing at home against the Rangers. There was some action in front of the Flyers net and a stick came up, went into the hole of Bernie's mask and got him right in the eye. Bernie had to retire after that injury.

Goalies today can take a puck at full tilt on the mask and not even blink. I think the masks today could stop a .45 Magnum. Every once in a while, a goalie will stick his head in front of a shot just for fun. But back when Tony played, masks were not as forgiving.

> **TONY:** A mask is not to stop you from being cut. A mask is designed for a goalie not to get hurt badly with broken bones and stuff like that. I've been cut while wearing a mask—just a fine cut that five or six stitches can fix, no problem. Now, with the big cages, you don't get cut but you have a tough time seeing the puck at your feet.

That's why the goalies today wear a mask more like Tony's, because they can see better.

* * *

Tony played with Phil in the 1972 Summit Series.

> **DON:** Now, the '72 series, that was something.

TONY: Yes, it was the greatest series because it was the first
time we played the Russians.

DON: What was it like?

TONY: Great.

I could see Tony didn't want to talk about it, so I moved
on to something else. When I talked to Phil about the
series in an earlier show, he had made an interesting
comment.

You have to remember that Team Canada lost the first
game in Montreal and the nation was shocked. Montreal's
Ken Dryden was in net for that game. The next game was
in Toronto, and if we lost that game—look out. So Harry
Sinden, the coach, put Tony in goal.

DON: You guys came back the next game in Toronto, and
[Wayne] Cashman played that game—and then
Harry benched him. I can't figure that one out.

PHIL: Cashman took down [Vladimir] Lutchenko with a
questionable hit—yes, he did. We had to intimidate those guys, but the reason we won in Toronto
was Wayne Cashman and my brother Tony was in
net. We won 4–1.

In the eight-game '72 series, Tony and Dryden split the
goaltending duties for Team Canada, with four games
each. Tony had the better record of the two (2–1–1), the

better save percentage (.882, to Dryden's .838), and his 3.33 goals-against average was better than either Dryden (4.75) or Tretiak (3.87). Tony won the game in Toronto and then had a tie in Winnipeg. So, he was undefeated in his first two games. In those two games, he gave up five goals, while Tretiak gave up eight.

Team Canada played three exhibition games before their first game in Russia. Tony was in net for Canada's only win, 4–1 over Sweden. Tony lost the first game in Moscow, but that was a gimme game—no way was Canada winning the first game in Russia. If they had lost Game 7 in Moscow, the Russians would've won the series. Tony went in net, stopped 31 shots and won 4–3, setting up Canada to win the eighth game. I wonder sometimes why Harry didn't go with Tony in Game 8. As a coach, you always go with a hot goalie.

* * *

In answer to the question of who is the greatest brother combination in the history of the NHL, everybody automatically says the Richard brothers. Henri "The Pocket Rocket" Richard and Maurice "The Rocket" Richard won 19 Stanley Cups between them, and the Rocket was the first player to score 50 goals in 50 games. The Rocket won the Hart Trophy in 1947, and Henri won the Bill Masterson Trophy (perseverance, sportsmanship and dedication to hockey) in 1974, and between them they had nine First-Team All-Star selections.

Are they the best brother combination in history? I have to say Phil and Tony are a very close second, if not tied for first. Phil led the NHL in goals for six consecutive years, winning the Art Ross Trophy five times; he was the first player to break the 100-point barrier, set the record for most goals in a season with 76 and won the Hart Trophy twice. Tony won the Calder Trophy for rookie of the year, the Vézina for best goalie three times, and set an NHL record for most shutouts by a rookie goalie. Between them, they won three Stanley Cups and were named to the First All-Star Team nine times. Both played a pivotal role in Team Canada beating the Russians in the '72 series.

I know if you look at the Stanley Cup totals, the Richard brothers win, but if you look at individual records, I'd say the Esposito brothers have the edge.

* * *

I remember the day we were trading Phil and Carol Vadnais to New York for Brad Park, Jean Ratelle and as he liked to call himself "the spare tire of the trade," a good little defenceman, Joe Zanussi. Phil was standing by a counter at a coffee shop eating a muffin and said, "Grapes, I'm going to do it your way, with shorter shifts." I thought to myself how ironic that he would say that now. Harry was in the process of trading him.

When I took over the Bruins I was warned: "Look out for that Esposito." So I went into the season with my eye on Phil, but I have to say Phil had his way of doing things, but as long as you were honest with him and didn't try and B.S. him, he was honest with you. He always had the team's interests at heart and really, nobody tried harder to win than Phil. His whole mission in life was to score goals and that was O.K. by me.

* * *

I'll add a little postscript about Phil and his life after hockey and how the Tampa Bay Lightning organization came about.

Gerry Patterson and a powerful restaurant chain owner had gotten together after the NHL had decided to expand in the 1992 season. We wanted to get a team in Hamilton, Ontario. The city had everything going for it. There was a new building, called Copps Coliseum, where season's tickets sold out in 17 minutes, and there was a lot of money behind the project and sponsorship deals at the ready. I was going to coach. It was a hockey-mad city.

There were some other teams in the running. Phil was trying to get a team in Tampa Bay and Bruce Firestone was trying to get a team in Ottawa. Both of those guys didn't have a building, money or anything.

The night before the NHL announced who was going to get the two expansion teams, Gerry went to a party and was told that we had the bid in our hip pocket, all set, no problem, it was ours. The next morning was the final meeting with the NHL. After that meeting, I could see by the look on Gerry's face that we had lost the bid for the team. Gerry didn't say a word and I asked, "Gerry, how can this be?"

Gerry shook his head and said, "Grapes, you wouldn't believe it. Phil walked into the room with the NHL, he had no money, no fans and no building. The NHL asked him about the building and Phil said, 'You want a building, you got a building.' They asked Phil about money and Phil said, 'You want the money, you got the money.' Whatever the NHL asked for, Phil, said, 'You got it.'"

Bruce Firestone saw Phil's song and dance and did the same thing. When it was our turn, our representatives (who had the money, the building and 14,000 season seats sold—we could have had 20,000 but the NHL capped it at 14,000) from the city of Hamilton didn't do what Phil had done, which infuriated Gerry. When they were asked about the money, they said to the NHL, "Can we talk about the money?" As soon as the NHL heard that, we were dead. After the meetings, the NHL announced the winning bids, Tampa and Ottawa.

We had everything and didn't get the bid, and Phil and Firestone, who didn't have a pot or a window to throw it out of, as they say, got an NHL franchise. So Tampa owes everything to Phil, he was the guy that got hockey in Florida.

Years later I asked Phil, "How did you get the money for the franchise?"

Phil said, "Well, Grapes, I went to Japan and when I talked to the Japanese businessmen and I asked them to invest their money, they thought I said Sake instead of Hockey."

He was kidding, I think.

BASEBALL

Fergie Jenkins, the first Canadian inducted into
the Baseball Hall of Fame.

LARRY WALKER AND FERGUSON JENKINS

MY FAVOURITE SPORT OUTSIDE OF HOCKEY is baseball,
with boxing a close second. I was a pretty good player in
my heyday, and my father played semi-pro ball in Kingston,
Ontario. I always root for the Toronto Blue Jays and Boston
Red Sox.

One of my all-time favourite players is Larry Walker from
Maple Ridge, British Columbia. The one thing I cannot
understand is why, with all he accomplished in his career,
he is not in the Hall of Fame. Of all the sports, the Baseball
Hall of Fame is the hardest to get into. When a player retires,
he has to wait five years to get on the ballot, and then he's got
10 years to get voted into the Hall of Fame. After that, he is

no longer eligible. Larry has been retired for 13 years, so only two more to go. Every year, members of the Baseball Writers' Association of America can vote for up to 10 players who are eligible, and a player must be picked on 75 percent of the ballots to get voted into the Hall. In the 2018 vote, Larry only got 34.1 percent. I hope he gets in, but it looks a little bleak.

Let's just take a look at Larry's stats:

* *National League MVP, 1997*
* *National League batting title, 1998, 1999 and 2001*
* *seven-time Gold Glove winner*
* *three-time Sliver Slugger winner*
* *best on-base percentage in the National League, 1997, 1999*
* *best slugging percentage in the National League, 1997, 1999*
* *66th in career home runs with 383*
* *.313 career batting average*
* *played in five All-Star Games*

There is something called the Hall of Fame Career Standards Test, which gives a player points for 19 different batting statistics. The average score of players in the Hall of Fame is 50, Larry scored 58.

I asked Canadian baseball writer Bob Elliott, who is in the Hall of Fame, why Larry is having trouble getting in. He feels it's because Larry played the majority of his career in Colorado, so he had an advantage in his batting statistics because of the altitude and thinner air. I find it hard to believe, but that's what he thinks. Not sure how playing in

Denver gave him an advantage in winning seven Gold Gloves, though. I just hope it's not because he's Canadian. Let's hope these writers get it right in the next two years.

The one Canadian who did make it to the Baseball Hall of Fame is Ferguson Jenkins from Chatham, Ontario. He was a big-league pitcher for 19 years and he played for the Philadelphia Phillies, Chicago Cubs, Texas Rangers and the Red Sox. In 1971, he became the first Canadian to win the Cy Young Award. The baseball writers got it right and inducted him into the Hall of Fame in 1991. We interviewed Fergie in 1984.

DON: Boy, it's great to have you on the *Grapevine*. I got to tell ya, I love it when I'm watching you on TV and the announcers say, "Ferguson Jenkins from Chatham, Ontario." It makes the heart feel good. Now, you come back to Canada in the off-season. How come?

FERGIE: Well, basically, when I first signed in 1962, I almost got drafted to go to Vietnam. I took a 12-month visa, which was basically the wrong thing to do. I should have gotten a 10-month visa. The Canadian government made a little stink about them trying to draft me. They wanted to classify me as draft-eligible, and if that happened I would have been in Vietnam in 1962.

DON: You'd be throwing hand grenades instead of baseballs.

I guess that is a pretty good reason to come back to Canada every year. I wanted to ask Fergie about what I think is the toughest thing in sports.

> **DON:** To me, the toughest thing in sports is this: bases loaded, two out, the count is two and two, and you throw a strike right down the middle and the ump calls it a ball. Now, you should be out of the inning and you have to calm down. How do you handle that situation?

> **FERGIE:** Well, I call the umpire Ray. He'll come and say, "My name isn't Ray." I'll say, "Oh, sorry. I thought you were Ray Charles, because if you blow a call on a pitch like that, there is something wrong."

I don't care what you say. With bases loaded, a 2–2 count, and you throw a strike and should be out of the inning and the ump blows it, it's got to be tough to settle down and throw another strike. Watch how many times that happens and the next pitch is either way outside or the guy hits it for extra bases.

JOSH DONALDSON AND BILL LEE

IN 2015, THE BLUE JAYS' JOSH DONALDSON was the best third baseman in baseball. When the fans were voting for the starters in the All-Star Game that year, Josh was well behind the Kansas City Royals' third baseman, Mike Moustakas. Every time I saw this mentioned during a Blue

Jays telecast, it really bugged me. If Josh were voted in as a starter, every player in Major League Baseball would know he was the best third baseman, but the reason he wasn't voted in was that he was playing for Toronto.

I asked my wife, Luba, where you go to vote for Josh. Then I made a sign that said:

WWW.TORONTO.BLUEJAYS.MLB.COM
JOSH DONALDSON
#VOTE BLUE JAYS

When she asked me what I was going to do with the sign, I told her I was going on *Hockey Night in Canada* to tell people to vote for Josh. She told me I was going to get into trouble—like that had never happened before.

So that Saturday on "Coach's Corner," while Ron MacLean just sat there, I went on the air to say my piece.

DON: Josh Donaldson, without a doubt, is the best third baseman in the world . . . among the 33 [third basemen] in the American League, he is first in homers, he is first in RBIs, he is first in runs, first in doubles and he is first in slugging percentage. Now, you're going to say he should be automatic [in starting in the All-Star Game], which really means a lot. . . . Now, what's happening in Kansas City, the guy there [Moustakas] can't carry Josh's glove, [and yet] he's got four million votes. You know why? The people of Kansas City voted, voted, voted. Now, I'm going to hold this up [I held up the homemade sign]. We cannot look bad in Canada, because if he goes down, everybody is going to say, "He's the best, but he played in Canada and they don't vote."

Well, Canada didn't let Josh down. When I did that "Coach's Corner," Josh had 2.3 million votes. Three weeks later, he had 14.1 million votes, more than any other player that year.

After that, the Jays contacted me and asked if I'd throw out the first pitch on Canada Day. The Jays were playing the Red Sox. I was to throw out the first pitch and Josh was going to be behind the plate. Now, could I be chicken and refuse? I almost did, but I'm glad to say I said yes.

I paced out 60 feet—roughly the distance between the pitcher's mound and home plate—and started practising. You'd be surprised how far 60 feet is. I realized that I had to throw the ball higher than in a normal game of catch and have the ball sink down, but even then, it's still a long throw. Then I tried it with my suit jacket on. My jackets are tight, and that made it even harder.

I was nervous and I wanted to get to the Rogers Centre, throw the pitch and get out. That never happens for me. First, I was taken to the umpires' room. They were getting the balls ready for the game. The umpires' room was so small I couldn't believe it, and they were eating cold pizza before the game. Some of the umps were from Boston and they wanted an autographed baseball. Now, I sign every-thing with a Sharpie marker—they write on just about everything. But the umps insisted that baseballs must be signed with a ballpoint pen. I guess all baseball people like their baseballs autographed with ballpoint pens, and not Sharpies, though Sharpies work and look a lot better. I was then taken to the Jays' locker room. I was introduced to a few of the Jays, but I don't think they knew me. All the ball boys and trainers, who are mostly Canadian, knew me. I met Josh and he thanked me for all the support, and then I met Blue Jays manager John Gibbons. He's a great guy.

I went out to the field, the Jays were still warming up, and I did an interview with Sportsnet's Hazel Mae. It was the first time I was on the Rogers Centre's artificial turf. It feels like you are walking on crushed cardboard. After the interview, everybody was getting ready for the national anthems.

Now my nerves started to kick in.

After the anthem was over, all the Jays were getting ready to go onto the field. The only Jay who I think knew who I was was José Bautista. He came up to me and joked, "Now help us get some pitching." I think what he meant was that I helped Josh get voted into the All-Star Game, and now I would be helping them out with their pitching.

The more I waited, the more I was getting nervous. Then the field reporter for the Red Sox came over and started to interview me, and I realized that all of my Boston fans would also be watching. I got even *more* nervous. If I just could have gone right onto the field and thrown the ball, I'd have been good, but all this waiting was brutal.

Finally, it was time. Josh came over and I said, "I'm really nervous."

Josh said, "Don't worry, I'll make you look good."

As I was walking to the mound, I was thinking, "How is he going to make me look good?" So I was standing at the mound and I looked around. The plate looked like it was a million miles away and Josh was crouched down like a catcher. I looked around, and there were 50,000 people, and the game was being broadcast back to Boston, and a lot of people were watching the Jays telecast.

The Blue Jays game announcer's voice boomed: "Okay, Grapes, it's your pitch."

I said, "Lord, please don't make me look like a fool."

I wound up and threw the ball, and I could see it was not going to make the plate. Josh got up from his crouch and started to walk towards the mound. He caught the ball in stride and kept walking. So now I knew what he meant when he said he would make me look good. I made it through thanks to Josh. But never again, say I.

As we walked off, someone from the Jays gave me the ball. They had put a little sticker on it with a code. They scanned the code with a machine. They went on to tell me that every first-pitch ball is marked with a special sticker and code and then is registered at the Hall of Fame so it can be identified if someone steals it or tries to sell it.

After that, I went up to the Rogers suite to watch the game. I was having a cold one—I needed one after that. Between the innings, I heard everybody laughing. I looked at the huge Jumbotron over centre field and it said, "Is this a Don Cherry jacket or a couch?" On the screen was a close-up of a piece of material, and you had to guess if it was one of my jackets or upholstery from an old couch. The people were killing themselves laughing. To tell you the truth, I got some of them wrong. I would see a piece of material and say to myself, "That would make a great suit," only to find out it was a couch. Lots of fun.

* * *

One of the first times I got into a similar situation was about 25 years ago. I got a call from the Toronto Argonauts, asking me to do the ceremonial kickoff at one of their games. I told them I had never kicked a football before.

They said, "It doesn't matter, the fans will get a bigger kick out of it if you screw up."

For a few weeks before the game, I practised, and I was brutal. The old saying "The more you practise, the better you get" didn't work for me on this. The more I practised, the *worse* I got.

The day came, and there were 20,000 fans at the Argo game. They placed the ball at the centre of the field. I remember Pinball Clemons was downfield and was going to catch the ball. Pinball was smiling—he's always smiling, come to think of it—or was he laughing at me? As I got ready and lined up for the kick, I said to myself, "Please, God, don't let me make a fool of myself." I tried to remember all the advice I had gotten over the past few weeks: Keep your head down. Don't look up. Concentrate on the ball.

Sometimes you think too much when you try and do these things—the golf pros call it "paralysis by analysis." But I was ready to do my best. I kept my head down, didn't look up, concentrated on the ball and gave it a mighty kick. It seems God was listening. When I did look up, the ball was spiralling down the field. It looked like I knew what I was doing. And then a funny thing happened. Pinball was about to catch the ball, and another player cut in front of him and caught it. I don't think Pinball was too happy. I walked off the field like it was no big deal, but inside I was repeating, "Never again, say I."

* * *

Last year, I got a call from a retired baseball player from Toronto named Greg O'Halloran. Greg told me that Ryan Dempster, the retired all-star pitcher for the Chicago Cubs (among other teams), wanted me to go down there and sing the late Harry Caray's favourite song, "Take Me Out to the Ball Game," at Wrigley Field during the seventh-inning stretch.

I asked, "Why does he want me?"

The Jays were in town and Ryan is from Gibsons, British Columbia, and he thought it would be great to have a Canadian sing the legendary song.

I thought, "Do I really need this?" Then I thought, "You chicken."

The tradition at Wrigley Field was that the Cubs' legendary baseball announcer, Harry Caray, would sing "Take Me Out to the Ball Game" during the seventh-inning stretch. Now, Harry would change the words a little. The one line in the song says, "For it's root, root, root, for the home team." Harry changed it to "For it's root, root, root for the Cubbies." I couldn't sing that—I am a Jays fan.

I was still hesitating, but I thought back to when I met Harry Caray at a Nike commercial shoot. It was a real thrill to meet him, and he was the nicest guy in the world. Harry knew a lot about hockey, and we had a nice chat about hockey and baseball. I thought it would be good to do it for Harry, so I agreed.

Now, my friend Bob Elliott was supposed to go along with me to Chicago. At the last minute, Bob said he couldn't make it, but that Greg would come along and bring a friend. So we got to the airport and there was a mix-up with the flights. It looked like we were not going to make it on time. Deep down, I was a little relieved, but then the Cubs' super pitcher, Jon Lester, arranged to fly us in on his private jet.

We got to Chicago and I wanted to check into my room and relax before heading to Wrigley Field. We got to the hotel and the front desk said, "Greg, we have two regular rooms for you and they are ready. Mr. Cherry, we have a special room for you, but it's not ready yet."

I said, "That's okay, just give me a regular room. We are in a hurry and I don't have time."

The front desk said, "Oh, no, Mr. Cherry, we were told to give you a special room."

I kept trying to explain that we had to get to Wrigley Field, but to no avail. So I had to go to Greg's room, have a shower, change my suit and rush out to Wrigley Field. We arrived in time to relax a bit before I had to sing. But then I made a classic blunder. Because the Jays were playing, Sportsnet was broadcasting the game back to Toronto. Someone from Sportsnet asked me to go onto the field and do an interview with Arash Madani. I stepped onto the Wrigley Field grass, which was pretty cool, and it had to be 100 degrees (Fahrenheit—I don't do metric), and with my suit, I was starting to melt.

I was walking by the Jays dugout and the players and manager saw me, and I kept thinking, "I can't say, 'Root for the Cubbies.'" So I told the equipment guys, "Tell the players I am going to say, 'Root for the best team.'" They laughed. I don't think they cared.

As I was walking off the field, one of the Cubs' PR people kept tugging at my sleeve. He pointed to the Cubs dugout. A guy was waving to me. It was the Cubs' great manager, Joe Maddon. He came over and said he was a big hockey fan and watched *Hockey Night in Canada* all the time. It was a thrill that he came over to say hello.

So I was led off the field and figured there would be an elevator to take us to the upper deck. But Wrigley Field was built in 1914 and, of course, they didn't have any elevators back then. Turns out they never bothered to put any in. So I had to walk up three floors. As hot as it was on the field, it was hotter in the stands with all the fans. The place was packed with Blue Jays fans, and they'd all had a few beers to cool off.

I took a million pictures, and by the time I got to the third floor I was soaking wet from the heat. The game started and I had to wait till the seventh inning before I sang. Again, I was waiting and I started to get nervous. I was told the organist, Gary Pressy, wanted to see me. He's a Bruins fan, and we talked about hockey and his father, who was in World War I and won a medal, and he showed me a picture of his dad. He said he was going to do something for me that he'd never done before: he was going to give me the key and start a little intro before I began to sing. This would help me because I wouldn't have to start "cold," as they say.

So I was still waiting for the seventh inning, and I started talking to a young man sitting next to me. Later, someone told me he was going to be the general manager of the Cubs one day. I asked, "Why do fans boo some of the people who sing during the seventh-inning stretch?" He said the last time someone got booed was the week before. He was a race car driver and they booed him because he said, "What a great place Wrigley Stadium is." It's Wrigley *Field*. I said, "Thanks, Lord." I was going to say Wrigley Stadium as well. I know better, but with everything that was going on that day, I forgot.

Top of the seventh, getting more nervous. The top half of the inning seemed to last forever. Then it was my turn. They introduced me, the organ master hit the key I was supposed to start in, and I started singing. It was easier than I thought.

The Blue Jays fans were out in numbers, but we lost in the ninth.

Back to the hotel. My special room was ready. They had put some beer on ice. Greg, his buddy and Ryan came over and had a few beers and we talked hockey and baseball. I explained how hockey players keep their beer cold by putting it in the sink or a bucket with water and ice. We finished the beer. I had a good time. I still thank the Lord for saving me again, but I am done with throwing out first pitches or singing at a ballgame. Ceremonial faceoffs are so much easier.

BILL LEE

EVERYBODY KNOWS THAT ALL GOALIES ARE a bit flaky. I have to say one of the flakiest (and I say that with all respect) guests we ever had on the show was pitcher Bill "Spaceman" Lee.

A southpaw, Bill played for the Red Sox from 1969 to 1978 and then was traded to Montreal, where he played for three years. The fans and media loved Bill. One of my favourite quotes from him was when he was asked about what he thought of mandatory drug testing. Bill replied, "I've tried just about all of them, but I wouldn't want to make it mandatory."

When Bill came on the show, he dressed the part as the free-spirited Bill Lee. He wore a lumberjack shirt, brown jeans, an old baseball cap and had a scruffy beard. One of the first things I wanted to ask Bill about was one of the greatest baseball brawls of all time. Now, most baseball fights or brawls are just pushing and shoving. But not in 1976 in a game between the Red Sox and New York Yankees.

> **DON:** I was in Boston when you were with the Red Sox, and I loved to watch you pitch. Any left-hander that can last in Fenway Park must be doing something right. Now, I want to ask you about the fight off the bat, that big fight between you and the Yankees. Give us the blow-by-blow of what happened.

> **BILL:** Well, that was a good fight. It was the first game against the Yankees in '76 since we won the

pennant in '75. Things were intense. Martin [Billy Martin, the Yankees' legendary manager] wasn't going to let anything slide. I had a 1–0 lead going into the seventh. There were runners on first and second and I gave up a base hit to Otto Vélez to right field. Dwight Evans picks it up clean and threw Lou Piniella out by 30 feet. Piniella slowed down coming home, but then he thought, "Billy Martin is the manager, I better make a show." He came home and really smacked [Red Sox catcher Carlton] Fisk. Fisk, dumb as he was, he took the hit straight on. He could have sidestepped him and flipped him if he wanted to. Instead, Fisk picked up Piniella, threw him down and smoked him with the ball. After that, it was Katy, bar the door. Next thing I know, Vélez is coming over the mound, and I grabbed him. Then I got smoked in the head by Mickey Rivers. Graig Nettles grabbed me. I was unconscious and he dropped me on my shoulder. I got up and my arm was numb. I thought, "Oh God, I don't think I can pitch the rest of this inning." Then I started yelling at Nettles. Jimmy Nettles [Graig's brother] and my brother played in Alaska together. So I was yelling at Graig, calling him everything in the book. I was yelling, "How could you do that to me, throwing me on the ground, grinding me into the ground, my bone poking me in the throat?" I tried to throw a punch at him, but my arm was like a piece of dead meat. He then smoked me again and down I went. Away things went again.

DON: After that, you turned into a—

BILL: A junkball pitcher. I call it a sanitation engineer pitcher.

There is one thing Bill and I had in common when we played. We both got in trouble with coaches and management after sticking up for teammates. I don't know how many times I got into trouble with my coach in Rochester, Joe Crozier, for sticking up for guys who were injured.

Bill was the same way. Bill's days in Boston ended when the Red Sox traded his friend Bernie Carbo. Bernie was a real free spirit, like Bill. He was a good player, and to Red Sox fans he will always be remembered for a game-tying pinch-hit home run in Game 6 that set up the famous Carlton Fisk walk-off home run against the Reds in the 1975 World Series. But the Red Sox management had had enough of Bernie's antics and traded him to Cleveland. Bill went nuts and called the management and owners gutless and called manager Don Zimmer a gerbil. Off to Montreal Bill went.

In 1982, he said he was going to protest the release of Montreal's second baseman, Rodney Scott, by having a one-game walkout. He was released and didn't play in the majors again.

DON: Bill, I'm not being smart or anything, but don't you see you got yourself in trouble for sticking up for your teammates. Do you ever get bitter at this? Do you think, "Next time I'm not going to do this, I'm going to think of myself"?

BILL: I can't do that. I never could. I believe in an upside-down or opposite pyramid. If you take care of everybody else, you will be taken care of. I do not believe in taking care of number one first. I've never been that way, and I always think that it's a reverse principle that gets things done.

When a guy puts his career on the line for teammates and friends, he's got something.

LARRY ZEIDEL

Larry "The Rock" Zeidel, my old roommate in Hershey.
Nobody fooled with the Rock.

THE TOUGHEST PLAYERS, PRESS CLIPPINGS AND
THE PROBLEM WITH ROOMMATES

WHEN I'M ASKED WHO THE TOUGHEST guys I ever played
against were, I think of three guys, and two of them were
my roommates.

The toughest guys were "Black" Tom McCarthy, a wild
Irishman with black, curly hair; Connie "Mad Dog"
Madigan, who I roomed with in Spokane; and my first
pro roommate and defence partner in Hershey, Larry
"The Rock" Zeidel.

Larry was one of the few Jewish players in the league.
From my understanding, his grandparents died in the
Holocaust.

Not so much today, but when I played, there were guys who were tough but you could play hard against them and drop the gloves and have a good go. Then there were guys you just didn't fool around with, and Larry was one of those guys. He wasn't one of those guys who would go out and do something to you for no reason, but if you did something to him or a teammate, look out.

He had no remorse.

I'll give you an example of why you didn't fool with the Rock. We were in Hershey and a rookie on the other team was starting to get on Larry's nerves. He would dump the puck in Larry's corner and say, "Go get the puck, Larry." Then he did it again.

I skated over to the kid and said, "Look, don't fool around with this guy."

He laughed and told me to get lost in so many words. Next shift, he came down the ice and dumped the puck in Larry's corner. Before he could say, "Go get the puck, Larry," the Rock took his stick and drove it right into the kid's nose. The guy went down and blood was pouring all over the ice.

Larry skated around and said, "Hey, why don't *you* go get the puck?"

As the player lay on the ice and Larry skated around, the other team didn't say a word because they knew: you don't fool with the Rock.

Before he spent 13 years terrorizing the minor leagues, he played two years in the NHL, and even won a Cup with the Detroit Red Wings.

DON: So, right off the bat, I've never asked you before, what were you making in Hershey?

LARRY: Well, I thought I was a National Leaguer because I played for the Detroit Red Wings, so I told Hershey I wanted an NHL-like contract. So I asked for seven grand.

DON: Seven grand! I was playing for three. Now, in 1952–53, you were in the NHL.

LARRY: Yes, I was with Detroit and won a Stanley Cup.

DON: Where's your ring?

LARRY: I got a plate.

DON: Didn't you get a ring?

LARRY: It was low-budget back then. I got a nice plate from Birks Jewellery.

DON: You didn't eat spaghetti off it, did ya? How did you end up in the minors with me?

LARRY: Well, I won the Cup in Detroit, and then the next year they shipped me off to Edmonton. I had a good year in Edmonton; we had a dream team: Johnny Bucyk, Al Arbour, Glenn Hall, Vic Stasiuk. I'm name-dropping now, but we all had a good year. I made the all-star team. It was all good. Then I started reading my press clippings. You should never read your press clippings. The papers said if Zeidel doesn't make Detroit, he'll be in New York—a good Jewish boy, a good fit with the Rangers, all that stuff. So I'm working hard in the summer on construction, getting ready for the season. One day, I'm having lunch with my little lunch pail, and I sit down and read the paper and it says, "Zeidel sold to Hershey." So, that's how I got to Hershey.

DON: So you come to Hershey. Did you know that you were responsible for Rose and me getting married? You get to Hershey and you're driving this big, beautiful light-blue Lincoln Continental. What a car. Rose and I were dating for a month or so and she sees you in this beautiful car. She thinks, "Hey, these hockey players are rich." So she chases me and chases me till she got me.

LARRY: I don't know about that. When I was rooming with you, you were playing all this love music, so she must have gotten to you. I'm trying to get ready for the game and you're playing love music.

DON: It was "Unchained Melody." Roommates? You never let me sleep.

LARRY: I tried, Don, I tried.

DON: I'd be coming in from the bars and you'd be going out for a walk. What was going on?

LARRY: I was always pumped up. I wanted to win so badly. You know how you walk racehorses after a race?

DON: You were supposed to go out and have a few beers.

LARRY: Don, you complained when I went for walks, took a bath or did anything, and I tried to be nice and quiet. Then you complained I breathed too loud. You said I kept you up all night breathing too loud.

DON: Well, you used to snore pretty good.

THE PENALTY BOX INCIDENT, JACK EVANS AND EDDIE SHACK

THERE ARE A LOT OF THINGS that I will remember about Larry, but there was one night in Cleveland that stands out in my mind. I got into it with a Cleveland defenceman named Ian Cushenan. Ian was from Hamilton, Ontario, and was a good six foot two and 190 pounds. We had a great go, and then we went to the penalty box. The same penalty box. All hell broke loose. Larry did something I'd never seen, before or since.

DON: Now, in Cleveland, I had a good fight with Ian Cushenan. Remember we wrecked the penalty box? The cops came into the penalty box and put a billy club right on my head. Now, I want to ask you: Why did you pick up the penalty box door and throw it on the ice?

LARRY: First, I want to say to everybody, you're really a good sport because before you got into a fight, you were like a matchmaker. You'd say, "You wanna go? Okay, let's go." In my day, if I talked to an opponent before I got into a fight, I caught more hell. In my day, you were just supposed to walk in and plant him one. So I got a kick out of you kids. I'm older than you. I thought, "Geez, these kids are really polite."

DON: You gave no warning. Just pow! Okay, now we went to the penalty box . . .

LARRY: Okay, now picture this: we go to the penalty box in our day, and they'd have a Pinkerton guard sitting there between the two combatants. So you have a go on the ice and you're still steaming and you're looking across at the guy, you know, you gotta get even. This poor Pinkerton guy is between you and that other guy. It's like a little phone booth. We got six guys—three players from one team and three players from the other team—sitting in a phone booth. The rumble starts and everybody is in the fight. The Pinkerton guy, he's down on the floor. It's so crowded the hinges come off the door and the door is laying on the ground. Now I'm fighting with this guy from

Cleveland and I trip over the penalty box's door that's on the ground and nearly get killed. I recover and I'm angry at the door and I don't want to quit. So I pick the door up and throw it on the ice, so now I can get back to the guy I'm fighting.

DON: Cushenan and I are going at it and we both stop and look at this guy picking up the door and throwing it on the ice. We both look at each other. He says, "This guy is nuts."

LARRY: The coaches gave us roles, didn't they? It's like a movie—some guys get the leading lady, some guys drive the getaway car and some guys get killed off early. My role was to go out there and balance the imbalance of intimidation. When the game starts, the one team wants to intimidate the other team because that's the easiest way to win, right? If you intimidate the other team, they'll quit.

Even before I met Larry in Hershey, I'd heard about him and how he was not afraid of using his stick to, as he says, "balance the imbalance of intimidation." Back in the 1952–53 season, Larry was playing with the Edmonton Flyers of the Western League, and in a game against the Saskatoon Quakers, Larry and a Quakers defenceman named Jack Evans got into it. I remember reading about it in the *Hockey News*.

Little did I know that, two years later, I'd be rooming with Larry.

DON: Remember the Western League? Remember Jack Evans?

LARRY: Oh, yes, I remember.

DON: Folks, I remember hearing and reading about this in junior—one of the toughest stick fights ever. Now, tell us what happened, and spare us nothing.

LARRY: Don, you know we all fell in love with the game when we were kids, either listening to Foster Hewitt or cutting out scrapbooks of your favourite player. You play minor hockey and then you sign with one of the big teams, you're 15 or 16 years old. Later, you go to training camp and you're like a puppy dog. When you go to camp, you don't know that those pros are tough, they're men. Then you scrimmage and they test you. They give you elbows, they run you, they train you to bark and bite. They tell you about guts and tell you to have a heart. So, I'm out in Edmonton. Now, in those days, the philosophy was each team had one scoring line and everybody else checked. You've got to have hitters to win championships. You gotta go out and try to intimidate that scoring line. Now, my coach came to me and said, "Larry, you're too emotional. The problem with you is that you let everybody in the rink know what you're doing. You're supposed to do it when the ref's not looking." Now, once in a while, you're skating up the ice, the ref's not looking and you either nick a guy with the stick or you get nicked. So, I'm skating up the ice and I get nicked with a stick. I always dropped the gloves and fought—sometimes it might be a sucker punch. So Jack Evans nicked me, he cut me. Well, he's not going to get away with that. So I swung back and missed. I swung my stick three times and missed three times. Now, this was my indoctrination on how to stick-fight.

DON: Did he miss?

LARRY: He didn't miss all three times. He took a chunk out of the top of my head, out of the bridge of my nose and one on my forehead. Now, when I was a puppy dog in training camp, the pros taught me that you gotta have guts and set an example for the rest of the team. I didn't go down. I was very emotional and they threw us out of the game. Now I'm frantic. I don't know what I look like and he doesn't have a scratch on him. He's smiling and the linesman is leading him off the ice. So I pick up a broken stick and I go behind him and used the stick to part his hair, but I eased up on him because I would have killed him. I go into the dressing room, and you couldn't see me for blood. They could have put a quarter in the hole on the bridge of my nose. I asked, "How are they going to stitch that one up?" That was my introduction to using the stick to defend myself.

* * *

After 13 years in the minors, Larry sent a letter to every GM in the NHL, telling them that he was ready to play and explaining how he could help their team. Sounds a bit crazy, but it worked. Larry made it back to the NHL with the expansion Philadelphia Flyers.

DON: Now you're 40 years old and you make it back to Philly in '67–68. How did you make it back to the NHL?

LARRY: Well, Bud Poile [the GM of the expansion Flyers] and I knew each other from Edmonton, where he coached me, and we won a championship out there. So I am with the Cleveland Barons and Bud shows up, getting ready for the expansion draft, and we go out for a few beers and he asks me to scout for him. So I'm playing for Cleveland that year and I write a report after every game. I told him to get Gary Dornhoefer [Gary was picked by Philly in the 13th round and ended up playing over 14 seasons] because I knew he had the stuff to win. So Bud flies me out to Philly before the expansion draft and I give him my opinion and he offers me a coaching job out in New Jersey in the Eastern League. But I still love the game. I told Bud, "I can still play. I've played against these guys for 10 years and I know all their moves." I kept at him, and then he gave me a shot.

DON: You came back at 40 and, playing on an expansion
team, you were a plus-17. Not bad.

When Larry was playing with Philly that first year, he
got into a brutal stick fight with Boston's Eddie Shack. It
was March 7, 1968, and the game was in Toronto because
the Philadelphia Spectrum was damaged in a windstorm
and the Flyers had to find a place to play.

Shack and Larry came together along the boards and
started to go at it with their sticks. They held nothing back.
There were photos of a bloodied Eddie and Larry splashed
all over the papers.

What many people don't know was that Eddie and Larry
had a feud going for over a decade. In 1958, at the Stamford
Arena in Niagara Falls, Ontario, Larry and Eddie first
went at it during an exhibition game between the New
York Rangers and the Hershey Bears. Larry and Eddie got
into it with the sticks and Larry was cut for 10 stitches.
They were both kicked out of the game. Then they went
at it again in the stands. The police got involved as well as
the fans. Larry, Eddie and Obie O'Brien got in trouble
and had to go down to the police station. Larry got a $200
fine for causing a disturbance.

* * *

Larry and I also played against each other. I was traded to
Springfield and we had a game against Hershey. The puck
went into the corner and I nailed a Hershey player pretty
good, and while I was standing over him, Larry came full

tilt, cross-checked me and broke his stick, right across my back. I went headfirst into the boards and got up looking to see who hit me.

Larry looked at me and said, "Donny, I lost my head."

I yelled, "If I get a hold of you, you'll lose your head, all right." But the refs got between us and nothing happened.

When I was coaching in Colorado, I got a call from Larry that he was in town and wanted to see a game. I got him two tickets right next to Rose and Tim. After the game, Tim took Larry down to see me in the dressing room and we talked for hours.

On the drive home, Tim was holding his side. I asked him what was wrong.

He told me, "Larry kept hitting me in the ribs every time the puck went into the corner and when there was a fight. My ribs are pretty sore."

Larry was just as emotional watching a game as he was playing it. He kept hitting Tim every time the puck went into the corner.

"If that was me or your dad, we'd put that player right through the boards," he kept telling Tim as he hit him in the ribs.

Larry retired in 1969 and stayed in Philly. He became a successful stockbroker. I know, reading about all the stick fights and blood, you might think, "What kind of guy is Larry Zeidel?" But that's what was expected of us when we played, and we didn't complain. I know it might be hard to believe after all you just read, but Larry was a really great guy who cared about and stuck up for his teammates.

KING CLANCY

Francis "King" Clancy did it all in hockey.
He was a player, coach and NHL referee.

THE MAN WHO DID EVERYTHING IN HOCKEY

IF THERE WAS ONE MAN WHO did just about everything that there is to do in hockey, it was Francis Michael "King" Clancy. Most people today remember King as the little guy that hung around with Leafs owner Harold Ballard. King Clancy was a player, a referee, a coach and then an NHL executive. We interviewed King in 1985. He was 82 years old, and it was less than a year before he passed on. He started off telling me he was a dog lover, just like I am. His dog had a funny name.

KING: Don, you know I have a dog too, and he's got a strange name.

A Bruins optional practice and everybody showed up.
That's Peter McNab being a wise guy with my hat.

After the '79 series, Scotty and I were offered contracts by our teams but we both felt it was
time to move on. Scotty went to Buffalo and I went to Colorado.

Phil scoring on his brother Tony in my first playoff behind the Bruins bench. Phil scored a hat trick and we won 9–2. Tony killed us the next two games and knocked us out of the playoffs.

Great shot of Phil Esposito in Game 5 of the '72 Series. Phil and Paul Henderson put Team Canada on their backs and won the series.

Scotty Bowman and Phil in Montreal during the '76 Canada Cup. Phil was mad at Scotty for not playing regular. Notice Phil has a black sweater on, meaning he was a Black Ace.

First pitch on Canada Day. Josh Donaldson made me look good.

Larry Zeidel and Eddie Shack, and the aftermath of their infamous stick fight at the Boston Garden. Eddie and Larry went at it years before in Niagara Falls.

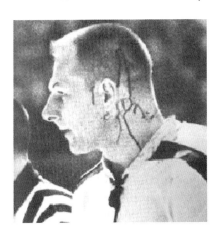

Francis Michael "King" Clancy in his heyday with the Leafs.

Me and Gord on the set of their video for "The Darkest One."

The Tragically Hip Way in Kingston, Ontario. I drive on this street every time I go to Wolfe Island, and I think of Gord and the boys.

Sunday, October 29, 1972

Can Don Cherry whip the Amerks into winners?

Yes, I did whip the Amerks into winners in just one year. That's goalie Lynn Zimmerman, Dave Hrechkosy and Wayne Morusyk in the background. Rose clipped this article out of the Rochester Democrat & Chronicle *and saved it in a scrapbook.*

DON: Really?

KING: Yes, his name was Sex. Now, that's a funny name to call a dog. Now, in that department I was okay years ago, but now, well, no dice. Anyway, one night he got loose and it was late, so I decided to go out in my pyjamas and look for him. So I went around the neighborhood, saying, "Here, Sex! Here, Sex!" Just then, a policeman drove by and stopped. He got out of his car and said, "What are you doing, King?" I said, "I'm looking for Sex." He said, "Not on my beat, you're not."

The crowd really laughed at that one.

* * *

King was born in 1903 in Ottawa and played his minor hockey in the Ottawa area with the Ottawa Munitions and Ottawa St. Brigid's. He turned pro in 1921 with the Ottawa Senators. He was one of the tough players (weren't they all), and even though he was a little small at five foot seven and 155 pounds, he never backed down.

King came from a family of good athletes. His mother was a good skater and his father was a football player with the Ottawa Rough Riders who got the nickname "King of the Heelers" because he could "heel" the ball back to the quarterback. In King's father's day, they didn't snap the ball back to the quarterback like they do today. The centre would stand upright and "heel" the ball back to the quarterback to start play. His father was as tough as they come, and he taught King a lesson about playing hockey.

DON: Your dad was a great football player and was one of the first imports to play in the CFL.

KING: That's right. They gave him the nickname "King," so later on they gave me the nickname King. I don't know why . . . I was just an ordinary player.

DON: You told me about when you got hurt one game and your dad was in the stands. You were on the ice and your dad yelled at you from the stands. What did he say?

KING: He said, "Get out of there." I said, "I can't get up. I'm hurt." He said, "Get up." So I struggled to my feet and got off the ice. I'll tell you who hit me. Rod Smylie—Dr. Rod Smylie of Toronto, here. He really corked me good.

DON: Was it a clean hit?

KING: Well, you know, clean or not, I guess it was all right. My dad said to me, "Get up off the ice." So when I went home, he said to me, "Never fall down like that." I said, "I was hurt." "That doesn't make any difference," he said. "You're never hurt. Get up. Don't give him the satisfaction." I said to him, "Dad, he gave me a pretty good shot." He said,

"Well, all you have to do is wait and give him one, and then you're all even."

* * *

King did just about everything in hockey. He played, coached, was an executive with the Leafs and an NHL ref. You can't do much more than that. But not only did King hold just about every position in hockey, he did something that never happened before or will ever happen again in a single game.

DON: In the 1923 finals, you played every position, including goaltender. How did that happen? Now, I can see you playing forward and defence, but how come you played goaltender?

KING: Well, Don, I'll tell you, we were playing in the Stanley Cup finals in Vancouver and our goaltender, Clint Benedict, who was the first goalie to wear a mask, took a shot at somebody, and of course Mickey Ion, who was the referee, sent him off. Back then, the goalies had to serve their penalties. I was the closest player to Clint, so he gave me the goal stick and said, "Here, kid. Take care of this place until I get back." I looked at him and said, "Are you crazy, dammit?" The next thing you know, they never got a shot on me and I got a shutout.

DON: That's better than what Hardy Åström [my goalie when I coached Colorado] ever did for me.

KING: You didn't have much in front of you in Colorado. Let's just say they were a little leaky.

DON: Leaky, all right, like the *Titanic*. I was the captain and I went down with the ship.

It's hard to believe nowadays that in King's time, and even when I played, teams only had one goalie. Sometimes when a goalie was injured, the trainer had to go in net. It does happen in today's NHL once in a blue moon. A few years ago, just before a game in Tampa, Carolina Hurricanes goalie Eddie Lack got sick so they had to dress equipment manager Jorge Alves as backup. Cam Ward was starting that night, but the Hurricanes let Jorge lead the team onto the ice for the warm-up. With seven seconds left in the game and the Lightning up 3–1, Carolina coach Bill Peters put Jorge in net. He didn't see any shots, but he can always say he played in the NHL.

Back in the day, some of the trainers weren't too bad when they played goal. It's hard to believe, but one made it to the NHL. It's the legend of Les Binkley.

Les was born in Owen Sound, Ontario. He played junior for the Galt Black Hawks in the Ontario Hockey Association and then knocked around the minors, playing in the Eastern and International Leagues for a while. In 1959, Les was playing for the Toledo Mercurys in the IHL. The Cleveland Barons of the American League called him and asked if he could make the two-hour drive up to Cleveland to play that night. Les arrived that night and he lost the game, letting in three goals, but he played well. The next season, the Cleveland Barons invited Les to training camp and offered him a job—not as the goalie, but as the trainer. I guess they were offering more money than Toledo, so Les took the job.

Les got a chance to show his stuff when the Barons' starting goalie, Gil Mayer, was hit behind the ear in a game in Buffalo. Les came in and played most of the game, but lost 3–2 to the Bisons. Les didn't get to play in any other games until late in the season, when Mayer was injured again. The Barons were in a dogfight for the playoffs with Buffalo and Rochester. Les played six of Cleveland's last eight games and ended up with a 4–1–1 record and a 1.44 goals-against average, helping Cleveland make the playoffs. The next season, Les was the Barons' starting goalie.

Les was no flash in the pan. He won the AHL rookie-of-the-year award in 1962, received two AHL All-Star nominations and in 1966 won the Hap Holmes Award for the best goals-against average in the AHL. Yet even with those stats, the NHL didn't come knocking. It was said that one of the reasons Les wasn't in the NHL was that he wore contact lenses.

But when the NHL expanded in 1967, Les became the number one goalie for the Pittsburgh Penguins and got his first win against the St. Louis Blues. Les went on to play five years in the NHL and four more years in the WHA.

Not bad for a guy who was a trainer.

My first trainer in professional hockey was Scotty Alexander. Scotty was the trainer for the Hershey Bears from 1945 to 1973, as well as the practice goalie, and he filled in for the Bears' goalie in a game or two. One game in Buffalo, our goalie was hurt late in the second period and couldn't start the third, so Scotty had to fill in.

The crowd was giving Scotty a hard time and he was givin' it right back to them. While he was yelling at the crowd, the knob on his goalie stick got caught in the net. Scotty was trying to get it loose, and he looked up and saw Sam Bettio on a breakaway. Sam was from Copper Cliff, Ontario, and a real sharpshooter; he scored 38 goals that year for Buffalo. Sam had played five years with the Bears, so he knew Scotty pretty good. As Sam was skating in on the breakaway, Scotty was frantically tugging on the stick, trying to get it free of the net. Sam zingered it home.

The crowd went nuts.

I remember that game because it was my first game back from one of my most painful injuries. Earlier in the season, I was taking a guy out in the corner. Our skates were made of leather, even the bottom of the boot. The blades were made from steel tubes and we didn't have that white plastic clip at the end of the blade that most of you would remember. It was pure, razor-sharp steel at the end of the blade. This guy's skate caught the bottom of my skate, and the razor-sharp steel end of his skate blade cut right through the leather and into the bottom of my foot. It was painful, but it got worse.

When I went to the dressing room and took my skate off, the blood was pouring out of my foot.

The doctor came, gave it a look-see, and said, "That's a pretty bad cut. We'll need to stitch it up." He rooted around in his doctor bag and started shaking his head, and then he looked up at me and said, "Sorry, son, but I forgot the novocaine, so I'm going to have to stitch the bottom of your foot with no freezing."

Needless to say, it was pretty painful. I missed a couple of weeks with that one.

Today, the Toronto Maple Leafs have a director of sports science and performance; director of rehabilitation; head athletic therapist; assistant athletic therapist; strength and conditioning coach; massage therapist; nutritionist; medical director and head team physician; orthopaedic physician; team dentists; and three equipment managers. But back when King and I played, the teams had a trainer like Scotty and a couple of stick boys. We did have team doctors, but they usually came the night of a game—and sometimes not even then.

When I was playing for Rochester, in a game in Quebec, I got a pretty good cut over my eye. The doctor wasn't in the building, so I had to go to the hospital to get stitched up. Believe it or not, there wasn't an ambulance in the building. I had to get a ride to the hospital. In my equipment, minus my skates, I got into a small Volkswagen bug and was taken to the hospital. It took about an hour to get stitched up, and then I headed back to the arena. I figured that the game would be almost over, so I would just get showered and then head out with the guys for a couple of pops after the game. I arrived back at the arena only to find out there had been a bench-clearing brawl that had gone on and on. When I got back on the bench, I had only missed about ten minutes of the game.

The lack of doctors meant we had to treat some of our "minor" injuries ourselves. Early in my career, I blocked a shot right on my knee. After the game, it was a bit swollen. I got on the bus and put ice on the knee. It bothered me for a few months, and I iced it after every game for the rest of the season. The next season, it was good to go, never bothered me.

Years later, I needed an X-ray on my leg after an injury. The doctor looked at the X-ray and asked when I had broken my kneecap. I told him I had never broken it, so he showed me the X-ray and sure enough, you could see where the kneecap had been cracked in two and healed up. I had played that whole year with a broken kneecap and never missed a game. That was our mentality back then: you just kept playing, no matter what.

When we had strains, we'd stand under a hot shower for a while. One of my teammates had a sore leg, so he got a rubber tube and connected it to a piece of rubber with holes in it that wrapped around his leg. He connected the rubber tube to the shower head and turned on the water and it would massage his leg. We all thought it was great until someone flushed the toilet and the shower water became scalding hot. He was screaming and he couldn't get the piece of rubber off. Needless to say, his leg was burnt very badly and the skin was peeling off when he finally freed his leg.

CONN SMYTHE AND RARE JEWEL

WHEN HOCKEY PEOPLE HEAR THE NAME King Clancy, they think of the Toronto Maple Leafs. But King started out his career playing nine years with the Ottawa Senators. At the start of his career, King was a phenomenon. He and his Ottawa teammate Hec Kilrea, uncle of the greatest junior coach Brian Kilrea, were the only players at that time to go from amateur hockey to the NHL before they turned 18 years old.

King was one of the most colourful players in the league, and in 1929–30 he had his best season for Ottawa. He was the Senators' top-scoring defenceman with 40 points. The next-highest-scoring Senators defenceman was Allan Shields, with nine points.

That season, the Leafs struggled. They were out of the playoffs and were well below a .500 club. The Leafs were filling a small arena called the Arena Gardens, also called the Mutual Street Arena, on Mutual Street (naturally) in Toronto. Maple Leaf Gardens was a year away from starting construction and Conn Smythe, part owner of the Leafs, knew they needed something to help the team start winning in order to fill the new Maple Leaf Gardens when it was finished.

Conn Smythe had his eyes set on King.

DON: Now, Conn Smythe, he was a great man.

KING: Yes, Don, he was a great man. His word was his bond. I never signed a contract with him all the years I played for the Leafs, some seven and a half years. Yep, never signed a contract. When he came down to Ottawa to sign me, after they bought me, I asked him for $10,000 and I thought he was going to have a stroke, but he gave it to me on a handshake.

DON: I can't figure it out—you got $10,000 in 1930 and I was making $4,500 in the 1950s. I don't understand that one.

KING: Well, I can tell you very easily. That's all you were worth.

The crowd really roared on that one. And he was right.

DON: There was a funny story on how he bought you from Ottawa, for $35,000, I think.

KING: Yes, it was $35,000 and two players, but one of the players had a broken leg, so it was mostly for the money.

DON: Thirty-five thousand dollars back in the '30s— that's a lot of money. Tell us how he got the money to buy you.

KING: Well, Mr. Smythe was in the horse business and he owned a couple of horses. I shouldn't say this because I'm not sure, but I think he used the money he made from the Marlboros and bet it on a horse called Rare Jewel. It won and made a nice little potful for Conn. So he decided the Leafs might want a hockey player to come from Ottawa, the land of milk and honey. When they were talking about buying me, I didn't think I wanted to come to Toronto. I had a job in the Canadian customs department, I was a big wheel there and I didn't spend much money. I was living at home with my mom and dad. I was single, so I didn't want to come to Toronto. My dad said to me, "I think you should go to Toronto." I said, "Why?" He told me, "I think Toronto is going to be the best hockey town in the country." And he wasn't wrong.

King's dad was smart; I'm betting he knew that Ottawa's time in the NHL was near the end. After the team sold King to the Leafs, it was put up for sale for $200,000 (that's about $2.7 million in today's dollars, a steal) but no one bit, so they shut down the next season.

I'll go into a little more detail about Conn Smythe and how he got the money to buy King. Conn did start buying horses in the late '20s, but nothing much ever came of it. A lot of hockey players seemed to like the horses. My goalie in Boston, Gerry Cheevers, owned a lot of horses, but he had a lot of success. Conn bought a filly named Rare Jewel for a couple hundred dollars, and the horse never won anything.

Then the horse's trainer, William Campbell, talked Conn into entering the horse in the 1930 Coronation Futurity Stakes. Now, no one knows how much Conn bet on Rare Jewel. The legend goes that he bet at the track and with bookies that worked out of the King Edward Hotel. Conn was a gambling man. In the late 1920s, Conn was owed $2,500 by the New York Rangers. He took the money and bet on a football game between McGill and the University of Toronto. He won, and on the next day he bet the $5,000 on a game between the New York Rangers and Toronto St. Pats. He won. In three days, he'd taken $2,500 and made $10,000. Today, that's about $140,000. Rumour had it that Conn took the money he made on the Toronto Marlboros junior hockey team and bet it on Rare Jewel. The Marlboros had just won the 1929 Memorial Cup and drawn sellout crowds at almost every home game.

Rare Jewel went off as a huge underdog and jockey Norman Foden, wearing blue and white silks, upset the field. A two-dollar bet paid $214.40, and Conn had bet at least $10,000, but many say it was a lot more. Conn knew he wanted King, but the Senators were asking $30,000 cash, and the other Leafs owners didn't want to pay that much money. Conn said he'd pay it out of his winnings from the race.

One last, strange twist to this story: on Wednesday, October 8, 1930, the Leafs held a press conference to announce they had an option to buy King Clancy from Ottawa and that the option expired on October 15. Conn put in the paper that he was going to let the fans decide whether the Leafs should go ahead with the deal. In that article, it went on to say, "the club will advertise in the newspapers asking the fans to express their opinion on the deal. Smythe says the club will be guided by what the fans say." I guess the fans said yes, but I think it was just a publicity stunt.

Can you imagine if Brendan Shanahan did that today with the Leafs? "Hey, Leafs fans, email or text me and let me know if I should trade for John Tavares."

KING, ACE BAILEY AND EDDIE SHORE

DON: Now, King, I was told you had a thousand fights and never won one.

KING: No, I won one.

DON: Which one?

KING: Eddie Shore.

DON: Eddie Shore!

KING: Eddie Shore, the toughest guy on the Boston Bruins. He was on his knees when I hit him.

When King played in the '30s it could be considered hockey's most violent era. In 1930, there was a game between the Boston Bruins and Philadelphia Quakers on, of all days, Christmas Day. The game was so out of hand that the ref and linesman needed help to get things settled down. An article from a Boston paper described the game like this:

Even the referee, Mickey Ion, and the linesman, Bill Shaver, took a couple of whacks on the chin before peace

*was finally restored by the gallant Boston Police, under the
stern supervision of Superintendent Michael Crowley. . . .
It was no Christmas for Philadelphia, which has managed
only one victory all season. They didn't even win any of the
fights on the ice. All in all, the 11,000 fans had a wild and
very merry Christmas at the Garden.*

I love the way the sports reporters wrote back then,
saying what everybody at the Garden was thinking. Today,
the write-up would have used the words "ugly incident"
about a thousand times.

* * *

Now, everybody knows about the rivalry between Montreal
and Toronto, but back in the '30s, Boston and Toronto had
just as vicious a hate-on for each other. One main reason
was that Leafs owner Conn Smythe and Boston's general
manager, Art Ross, had a major feud.

KING: You know, I played many times up in Boston. Some
nice, quiet games.

DON: You played against Shore.

KING: Oh, a nice, quiet guy.

DON: You were there with Ace Bailey.

KING: I was responsible for that whole thing.

DON: I never read that; tell us about what happened.

KING: Well, I was going into the Boston end with the puck; how I got there, I'll never know. Shore tripped me. He's got the puck now and he's coming in on our defence. I said to him, "Come back here again, I'm waiting for you." Shore said, "I'll be right back." Of course, Shore could have eaten me, you know, but not as long as I had the stick.

DON: The old equalizer.

KING: So he did come back and I gave him a knee and Shore went flying. Now Bailey picked up my position on the right side and Shore hit him in the forehead and sent him flying, and Bailey hit his head on the ice. Red Horner came off the bench, and they say the game is rough today, he corked Shore right in the nose and he was flatter than you-know-what on a plate.

DON: That was almost it for Ace.

KING: That was it for Ace. He never played again.

It was December 12, 1933, and the Leafs were at Boston Garden. The game was pretty rough from the get-go. One Boston paper said even before the incident, "The Garden was soaked with Eddie Shore's blood. He was taking a terrible beating from the Toronto sticks while he was guarding the Boston net, trying to aid Tiny Thompson."

As King said, he was carrying the puck up the ice and Shore hit him and knocked him off the puck. Shore then carried the puck down the ice, where King gave Shore a knee and sent him flying. King then changed and Ace came on, playing right defence. The play went back up the ice towards Boston's end, and Shore was behind the Leafs defence. I guess Shore had had enough of the Leafs and thought it was Ace that had hit him. The play was coming back to the Toronto end, and Ace was skating backward with his back towards Shore. Shore roared up the ice, hit Ace from behind and sent him flying. Bailey hit his head on the ice.

It was said you could hear his head crack all over the Garden. He was bleeding and went into convulsions. The play stopped and Shore went to the boards along the blue line as they attended to Ace.

Leaf defenceman Reginald "Red" Horner jumped on the ice, skated over and said to Shore, "That was a dirty check, Shore."

Shore just smiled at him, and then Red cold-cocked Eddie.

Red was six foot one and 200 pounds and was as tough as they come. Shore was knocked cold, and his head hit the ice as well. When Shore hit his head, it cut him from the top of his scalp to the nape of his neck. He came to and was carried off the ice in a stretcher.

With Ace, the doctors thought he was dead. It was said that after the convulsions on the ice, he started to turn blue. He came to for a minute and then faded again and was taken to Audubon Hospital in Boston. The doctors feared that Ace wouldn't last the night.

After the period, tensions were high and Conn Smythe started to get into it with some Bruins fans. One of the Bruins fans said Ace was faking it and Conn drilled him and cut him over the eye, shattering the guy's glasses. As more Bruins fans went after Conn, King and some of the other Leafs came to his rescue, and again King used his stick as the big equalizer.

The next day, Conn had to go to court and plead not guilty to assault and battery and was released on a $100 bond. I guess the charges were dropped.

I don't know how true this is, but it's been said that when Ace's father heard about his son's injury and how it happened, he jumped on a train headed for Boston with a loaded gun in his pocket. The story goes that Smythe heard about what Ace's father was up to, so he contacted Frank Selke, who called a friend on the Boston police force. Ace's father was found in the bar the Leafs frequented in Boston and was convinced to give up the gun and go home.

There were rumours going around that if Ace died, Shore would be served a warrant for manslaughter. When asked about this, an inspector on the Boston homicide squad, John F. McCarthy, said he interviewed Shore and after the interview he felt there was no criminal intent. But to this day, many think that Shore did what he did because King knocked him down and the Leafs were giving him a hard time all game. Shore gave this statement to McCarthy:

I was skating along with my head down. I figure I was
traveling at a speed of 22 miles per hour. I saw Captain
Marty Barry of the Bruins coming with the puck and I
was skating fast to get out of the zone before an offside was
declared. I didn't see Bailey until it was too late. My left
side struck against his left side. I don't remember whether
I was knocked down or not. There was no feeling between
us. I wasn't carrying the puck. Harry had it. It was purely
accidental." (Port Arthur News, *December 15, 1933)*

A few days later, Ace was moved to another hospital
and had two operations to relieve the pressure on his
brain. After the second one, the doctors didn't think he
was going to make it through the night. A priest was called
in to give Ace the last rites. The next day, Ace started to
rally, and after a few weeks the doctor said he was going
to live.

The funny thing was that Leafs management didn't
blame Shore. Like I said, Art Ross and Conn Smythe had
a feud going. But Smythe was quoted in the paper as
saying, "Shore is one of the finest sportsmen I ever met. I
don't blame him for the accident which may cause the
death of Bailey." He went on to blame the Bruins' coach
and management for the fighting.

Ace's playing days were over. So on February 14, 1934,
the Leafs played a team of NHL all-stars, with the gate
receipts going to Ace. The all-star team was made up of
greats like Lionel Conacher, Ching Johnson, Aurèle
Joliat, Bill Cook and the great Howie Morenz, who got
the goal of the night. Eddie Shore was also on the team.

The Leafs won 7–3, with the Leafs' Baldy Cotton—from Nanticoke, Ontario—scoring what turned out to be the first goal in an NHL All-Star Game. The highlight of the night was when Ace, dressed in street clothes, met Shore at centre ice and the two shook hands. The crowd gave them a standing ovation.

After that, Conn Smythe took the microphone and he announced that "no other player on a Maple Leafs hockey team will ever wear the number 6 again."

That was the first number the Leafs retired. The first number any NHL team retired, in fact.

Ace was presented with a cheque for over $20,000 from the gate that night and the Bruins kicked in a cheque for $6,000 they had raised for Ace.

KING REFEREEING IN BOSTON AND THE FIRST TIME I MET KING

IN BOSTON, NOBODY WAS SAFE FROM the Gallery Gods—the fans that sat in the very upper balcony of the old Boston Garden. They would be hanging right over you, and nobody escaped their wrath.

> **DON:** You told me that when you were a ref, you loved doing games in Boston.

> **KING:** Well, I don't think they liked me that much. Before one game, I was standing at attention when they marched the flag out onto the ice before the anthem. With the flag, they had two soldiers with

rifles march out. It was all quiet before the organ started playing and some little guy from the Gallery Gods yelled out, "Hey, when the anthem is over, before you leave the ice, shoot Clancy."

DON: You gotta love those Gallery Gods.

KING: The next game, just before the game got started, it was again all quiet, and I think it was the same guy, he yelled, "Hey, Clancy. We want to let you know we named a city in Massachusetts after you." Well, I thought, "What a nice thing." I gave him a wave, and he yelled, back, "Yeah. It's called Marblehead."

I enjoyed having King on the show. The first time I met him was at training camp. Of course, he was with the Leafs organization and I was with the Rochester Americans of the American Hockey League. I have often said that most of the people with the Leafs—well, most NHLers at the time, including a lot of the players—would look right through us American Leaguers as if we were ghosts. But not King. He would come over and say hello to you and shake your hand. That might not sound like a lot, but it meant a lot to us players in the minor leagues. I'll remember King for that.

GORD DOWNIE

Me, Bobby and Gord at a Leafs vs. Bruins game at the ACC.
We talked about the Bruins, hockey and had a good laugh.
This was the last time I saw Gord.

REMEMBERING A FRIEND

I CONSIDER GORD DOWNIE A FRIEND of mine. Everybody
thinks Gord was born in Kingston, Ontario, but he
was born just outside Kingston in a township called
Amherstview. My brother Richard was a principal in one
of the schools that Gord went to and used to see him
play street hockey all the time. Harry Sinden, my general
manager in Boston, is Gord's godfather.

Gord loved hockey and he loved the Bruins. When
he was young, he played goal for the Kingston AAA
team. Gord always had songs about Canada and about
hockey. "Fifty Mission Cap" talks about Bill Barilko
and his Stanley Cup–winning goal. "Fireworks" talks

about watching Paul Henderson's goal in '72 and mentions Bobby Orr. In the album *World Container*, there is a song called "Lonely End of the Rink." The song "Heaven Is a Better Place Today" is about the 2003 death of NHLer Danny Snyder.

He also wrote a lot about Kingston. The song "Skeleton Park" is about McBurney Park, which began to be called Skeleton Park by the people in Kingston after it was discovered that it used to be a cemetery. I used to play ball in that park all the time.

To tell you the truth, the first time I heard about Gord and the Tragically Hip was through my mechanic, Jay Miller. He is one of the millions of Hip fans. I soon found out that, like most Hip fans, he was loyal and a fanatic.

In 1998, the Hershey Centre opened in Mississauga, which is where my OHL team, the Mississauga IceDogs, played. On February 19, 1999, the Tragically Hip were to play the Hershey Centre on their *Phantom Power* tour. I got a call from the band's manager and was asked if I would like to introduce the band when they went on stage.

Before the show, Ron MacLean, who is also a big fan, and I went down to meet everybody. We met the band and took pictures with Rob Baker, Paul Langlois, Gord Sinclair and Johnny Fay, and Gord was off to the side by himself. You could see that he had a goalie's mentality. He was alone, getting ready for the show. In many ways, Gord was like the band's goalie. Even if the rest of the band had a great show and Gord had an off night, everyone would say the band had a bad show. The same as a goalie: you can have a good team, and as a coach, you can have your team ready, but if your goalie has a bad game, the chances are you're going to lose.

Just before the band came on, I walked out and said something like, "Here they are, from my hometown of Kingston, Ontario, my buddies the Tragically Hip." They came on stage and started to play "Something On." Ron and I went up to a box at the Hershey Centre. By the time we got to the box, they were playing "Courage (for Hugh MacLennan)" and they were in full swing. The sellout crowd was going nuts. It was the first time I had seen Gord perform, and I have to say I couldn't take my eyes off him. It was incredible how he commanded the stage. Full of confidence, and he never stopped. They ended the night with "Fifty Mission Cap." I'm not sure, but I was told that was the only time the band was introduced before they went on stage.

The next "Coach's Corner," we talked about Gord and the Tragically Hip. Not too long after, someone at the CBC contacted me and asked if I wanted to present an award on the Juno Awards show. I didn't even know what the Junos were for. They told me I would go on stage with Gord, say a few words, hand out the award, and that was it. So, knowing Gord was going to be there, I said sure. I got to the show and they told me Gord had had to cancel and I was to present the award with a Canadian opera singer named Measha Brueggergosman. She is pretty tall and had heels on; she looked as tall as Zdeno Chára. I looked like a hobbit next to her. We presented the award; I was awful.

* * *

A few years later, I got a call and was asked if I would be in a Tragically Hip video for a song called "The Darkest One." Along with the Tragically Hip, the guys from *Trailer Park Boys* were going to be in it. It sounded like fun. They were shooting at night, some place north of Mississauga. I got the directions, but ended up getting lost. I was on a two-lane road and couldn't find the road I was supposed to turn off on. I went down a dirt road, almost a path, and it opened up into a real trailer park. When I arrived, I remember it was freezing cold and the director told me to wait in a pickup truck and that they'd call when they were ready for me.

He explained the story behind the video: the Trailer Park Boys steal an engine for Gord in exchange for some booze and a bucket of chicken. I was the chicken delivery guy and was to deliver two buckets to the trailer. Gord would bring the buckets inside the trailer, and a bunch of cats would eat it, so they'd order some more. When I arrived again, they didn't have enough money to pay me. That was the gist of the video.

While I was waiting in this truck, Gord hopped in. He was wearing a black knit cap pulled down; I didn't recognize him at first. We talked a bit about the Bruins and hockey, but I could see something was bugging him. Then he started to apologize about cancelling on me and told me how bad he felt when he saw me at the Junos.

He said, "When I saw you on the show, I felt so bad."

I could see it was really bothering him, and I just laughed it off.

Finally, they were ready to shoot. I was to drive up in a red Ford Pinto with a big chicken on the roof. I don't think the engine even worked—the film crew pushed me down a hill. The brakes barely worked and I almost had to put my foot through the floorboards to stop. I went up to the trailer and gave Gord the chicken, and he gave me the money. The great thing about it was that the money was old money—he even gave me a two-dollar bill—and they were drinking beer out of stubby bottles. All the while, the band was playing in the trailer.

The next scene, I was to come back with another two buckets of chicken and give it to Ricky, Julian and Bubbles. They didn't have enough money and we were supposed to argue. The director yelled, "Action!" I gave the chicken to Bubbles and Ricky gave me the money. I started to push Bubbles, and he started to push me back. Then I started pushing Ricky. Julian knocked my cowboy hat off and I slapped the cigarette out of his mouth. We kept pushing and shoving and grabbing each other. All the while, the band was playing in the trailer window. Bubbles, Ricky, Julian and I were really going at it. The director yelled cut. I walked away and gave Julian one last good shove. I think we did it in one take.

It turned out great. You can't get more Canadian than the Trailer Park Boys, the Tragically Hip, old money, stubby beer bottles and me.

* * *

I was really upset when I heard about Gord's health. He is one of Canada's biggest rock stars of all time and he reminds me of a young hockey player—down to earth, as humble as humble could be. I don't know the music business all that well, but I heard that the guy that writes the song makes more money than the rest of the guys in the band. Gord wrote most all the songs, but he wanted everything split down the middle. They were a team. A hockey team. That's the kind of guy Gord was.

They launched a farewell tour in the summer of 2016. Their last concert was in Kingston, at the K-Rock Centre. The arena is located at 1 The Tragically Hip Way. I was nervous for the band and Gord. I can't imagine the pressure on them to perform with all of Canada watching. I mean, the country stood still for this concert. Now *that's* pressure. Ron was in Rio for the Olympics and did his usual great job. The whole show was a smashing success.

Four months after that final concert in Kingston, I got a call from Bobby Orr. He had a box at the Air Canada Centre for a Saturday night game between the Leafs and Penguins, and Gord was going to be there. I told him I'd head over after I did "Coach's Corner," since the *Hockey Night in Canada* studios are in the CBC building a few blocks away from the ACC.

When I arrived, there was Gord in a knit cap and a jean jacket with a poppy. I congratulated him on the tour and the last show in Kingston. Bobby, Gord and I talked about the Bruins and hockey and had a few jokes. I couldn't stay too long as I had to head back to the studio.

As I was leaving, Gord gave me a hug and a kiss. He looked me in the eye and said, "Goodbye, Don."

That was the last time I saw Gord.

As you might know, I have a cottage on Wolfe Island,

across the St. Lawrence River from Kingston. To get to the island, you have to take a ferry. To get to the dock you have to drive down The Tragically Hip Way. When I go to the cottage, I always think of Gord.

BOBBY HULL

Bobby Hull and me on set. Bobby was the first player to score
more than 50 goals in a season.

TWO NHL RECORDS ON ONE GOAL AND
THE FIRST CURVED STICK

ONE THING THAT SEEMS TO HAVE gone by the wayside in
the NHL is good nicknames. If I had to pick the best, it
would be a tie between Maurice "The Rocket" Richard
and "The Golden Jet," Bobby Hull.

I don't think Bobby Hull gets the recognition he
deserves for how great a goal scorer he was when he played
for the Chicago Blackhawks. Just like Phil Esposito, when
people talk about the greatest goal scorers in the history of
the NHL, Bobby doesn't get his due.

Everybody knows that 50 goals in a season is the gold
standard for players. When a player is off to a good start, the

question will come up of whether he will hit the 50-goal mark. Of course, the Rocket was the first player to score 50 — the only player to do so in the NHL's first 43 seasons — and then Bernie "Boom Boom" Geoffrion was the second, in 1960–61. And then came Bobby Hull, in 1961–62.

After Bobby did it, the NHL took a leap forward. On March 12, 1966, the Hawks were in Chicago, playing the Rangers. The Rangers jumped out to a 2–0 lead. Bobby Hull got an assist on a goal by Stan Mikita, and then later, on a power play, the glass ceiling of 50 goals was broken. Bobby tied the game at two when he stepped over the blue line and let one go. He had scored his 51st goal, making him the first person to ever score *more than* 50 goals in a season.

What most people don't know is that Bobby's goal set two NHL records: the first being the most goals ever in an NHL season, while the second was the most power-play goals by a player in a single season. Bobby had scored his 21st power-play goal, surpassing Camille "The Eel" Henry's record of 20.

When we interviewed Bobby, we were shooting the show in the CHCH studio in Hamilton, Ontario. We had decorated the set with hockey stuff, and one of the items hanging on the wall was a stick with a plaque on it that read "Bobby Hull: 50th goal 1968–69." I thought it was just a prop, but when I looked at it more closely, I could tell it was a game-used stick.

The first thing I noticed when looking at the stick was the curve: it looked like a banana. It sure looked like a stick Bobby Hull would use. When I asked around about it, Ralph Mellanby, the executive producer of the show, said he'd had it for years and didn't remember who gave it to him. But I was pretty sure that this was the actual stick Bobby used to score his 50th goal in the '68–69 season.

> **DON:** Before we get started, I have something for you. This is the stick that you got your 50th goal with in the 1968–69 season.

> **BOBBY:** That was one they were supposed to give back to me from the Hall of Fame. But for some reason, they didn't return it to me.

> **DON:** Well, Ralph wanted me to give it to you, so you got it now. Now, I want to ask you about the curve. How did that—

> **BOBBY:** I'm not guilty. It was Stan Mikita. Stan had the terrible habit that if he didn't like a stick, he would just lean on it and break it. I said to Stan a hundred times, "There are 400 little guys out there that would just love to have your stick. Instead of breaking it, hang it on my rack and I'll make sure someone gets it." One day, he didn't like a stick, so he tried leaning on it but he couldn't break it. He didn't have enough weight— it was late in the season. So he went over to the bench door and rammed the stick in between the hinges. He pulled on it and pulled on it and the blade split in two. The top part flew off and the bottom part stayed. So the stick had a big curve. So he's skating off the ice and he takes a puck, and with the broken stick snaps it into the net. Now, I'm watching him. He

circles back, fishes the puck out of the net, and then fires it back into the net. Now, he did this six times. I said to the guys (we were down at the other end of the ice), "Look at Mikita, he's gone cuckoo, look at what he's doing." I went over to Stan and said, "What are you doing?" He said, "Bobby, I tried to break my stick and I put a hook on the blade, and boy, can you ever fire the puck with it." So after practice, Stan called Northland [that's the make of stick he used] to get them to make a few sticks with a curve in the blade. Stan ordered me a half a dozen as well. From there it went from a little curve to a huge curve.

Towards the end of Bobby's career, you wouldn't believe the size of the curve on his stick. It got so crazy with the curves, widely called "banana blades," that the NHL had to institute the "Bobby Hull rule" and limit the size of the curve. In 1967–68, the league limited the curve to an inch and a half. Two years later, the NHL cut that back to one inch. In 1970–71, they settled on half an inch. And that's where it stayed until 2005–06. The following season, they eased up and set a limit of three-quarters of an inch.

* * *

When Bobby went soaring down the left wing with his blond hair flying (hence the nickname the Golden Jet) and he started to wind up, there was true fear in the hearts of the goalies.

DON: Let me tell you about Gerry Cheevers [my goalie when I coached the Bruins], and this is a true story. The Hawks had a power play, and you had a player just sift the puck over to you and you wind up and hammer it. He'd be ducking out the way, hoping you score. You did this five times on the power play, and the fifth time you hit the crossbar and it went into the crowd. Gerry came to the bench and I said, "Geez, Gerry, those pucks almost hit you." He said he never prayed as hard that someone was going to miss the net.

BOBBY: Yeah, that's true. There was another time I got the puck out at the point. One of the Bruins came running out and I wound up, he went down to block the shot and I stepped around him. I walked in about 10 or 15 feet and wound up again. One of the Bruins defencemen came out and slid to block the shot. I managed to slide around him and walk in again, and then I'm about 20 feet from the net. So I wind up again and I look up, and the net was vacant. I start to laugh, and there was Cheevers, hiding behind his other defenceman—and I put it in the open net.

The goalies *were* afraid of Bobby's slapshot. Their equipment provided little protection against a shot like Bobby's. Some goalies back then still didn't wear a mask.

Bobby was the third hockey player to be on the cover of *Time* magazine. The first was Lorne Chabot in 1935, and the second was a painting of Ranger goalie Dave

Kerr in 1938. And then they featured a painting of Bobby Hull in 1968 with the caption CHICAGO'S BOBBY HULL, FASTEST SHOT IN THE FASTEST GAME.

When he wound up, everybody was afraid. He was the first player to have his slapshot clocked at over 100 miles an hour. And that was with a wooden stick. Can you imagine what he'd do with a modern composite stick?

But Bobby had another weapon as well.

> **DON:** You liked the wrist shot as well as the slapshot, didn't you?

> **BOBBY:** I think I scored about 50 percent of my goals on the wrist shot. Then, when I went to the WHA, I think I scored more goals on the wrist shot than slapshot. For any kids watching, that's the bread and butter shot. Get the puck, get it away quickly onto the net and don't telegraph your shot.

For all you kids or coaches reading this, both Phil Esposito and Bobby Hull, two of the greatest goal scorers in the history of the NHL, say the same thing: get your shot off quick.

THE WHA AND THE 1976 CANADA CUP

IN 1972, BOBBY'S CONTRACT WAS UP with the Blackhawks. At that time, the NHL was still not paying its players all that well, especially the stars. There were rumours that the World Hockey Association—the new league that was forming to compete with the NHL—were looking to get a big star to jump to their league, and Bobby Hull's name came up. When asked in the press what would it take for Hull to jump to the WHA, he joked, "A million dollars." So the owners of the WHA got together and each threw about $100,000 into the pot to get Bobby to sign with the Winnipeg Jets. The Jets would sign Bobby to a 10-year contract worth over $1.5 million, along with a million-dollar signing bonus. That may not sound like much now, but back in 1972 it was an unheard-of amount of money.

DON: You got to admit, it was a mistake leaving Chicago to go to the WHA.

BOBBY: Well, I never look back, and it's not the City of Winnipeg, but I spent 15 years in Chicago. It's one of the greatest cities with some of the greatest fans you'd ever want to meet. But the Hawks backed me into a corner and I made a decision to go to Winnipeg. Taking everything into consideration, all the money and everything, I would have been better off playing in Chicago.

DON: You could have run for mayor there and won easily. You were the first guy to get the big dough, but the WHA threw things [salaries] out of whack.

BOBBY: The WHA was necessary because the NHL was blocking professional hockey in different areas of the country that deserved it. Now, take a look at the strong franchises in the NHL because of the WHA. Edmonton, Winnipeg, Quebec . . . Look at Edmonton: five years in the NHL and they win a Stanley Cup.

The WHA folded in 1979, and four teams merged with the NHL: the Edmonton Oilers, Quebec Nordiques, Winnipeg Jets and New England Whalers. New England became the Hartford Whalers and then moved to Carolina in 1997 to become the Hurricanes.

Bobby did pay a price for jumping to the WHA. He was not allowed to play in the 1972 Summit Series. Team Canada had to take on the Russians without two pretty good players named Bobby: Hull and Orr.

The first Canada Cup took place in 1976, the first real best-against-best tournament. This time, Team Canada had both Bobbys playing on it.

DON: Now, that '76 team may be the greatest team ever.

BOBBY: You were there, Don, with Scotty [Bowman], Al MacNeil and Bobby Kromm. Do you know why it was the best team Canada ever iced? Because one Number 4, Bobby Orr, played on it. He didn't have a chance to play in the '72 Series. On one leg— without a word of a lie, when he came off the ice, his [bad] knee would be twice the size of the other knee. He'd spend an hour with ice bags on it just to get the knee's swelling down. On one leg, he was better than the rest of us would ever have thought of being.

DON: He is the greatest.

BOBBY: We had some pretty good defencemen too. Serge Savard, Guy Lapointe, Larry Robinson, Denis Potvin, Paul Shmyr. That team was just unreal.

How did the two Bobbys do in the 1976 Canada Cup? Well, Bobby Orr won the tournament MVP and tied for the scoring lead with a Russian and Denis Potvin with nine points. Bobby Hull led all Team Canada forwards with five goals and three assists in seven games. That makes you wonder if the 1972 series would have been as close as it was if both Bobby Orr and Bobby Hull had played in it. In fact, the Russians finished with a 2–2–1 record in the 1976 Canada Cup and didn't even make it to the finals.

AUTOGRAPHS AND BOBBY'S BROTHER DENNIS

LIKE I SAID, WHEN HE WOUND up for a slapshot, nobody's shot was as feared as Bobby Hull's. His brother Dennis struck fear in people too. If you were at a speaking engagement, your biggest fear would be following Dennis Hull, maybe the greatest dinner speaker of all time. He's made a living out of poking fun at himself and his big brother Bobby.

Dennis was a good player in his own right. He played on Team Canada 1972 and played for the Hawks for 13 seasons.

DON: Your brother Dennis, he is something else. One of the best dinner speakers of all time.

BOBBY: One time in Belleville, my dad was walking down the street, and someone came up to him wanting to know the inside scoop of the Blackhawks and said, "Hey, Mr. Hull, what's the latest dope in Chicago?" My father said, "My youngest son."

DON: Yeah, Dennis wasn't too bad. His best year, he had 40 goals. From 1970–71 to the '72–73 season, he had over a hundred goals.

BOBBY: If they would have given him a straight chance in Chicago, he would have been as good as anyone, but in Chicago they thought just because his last name was H-U-and-two-sticks that he should play like his brother.

DON: They booed him in Chicago.

BOBBY: On the road, he was our best player. He scored most of his goals on the road.

DON: He gets the puck in Chicago, he rifles it home and they'd give him the Bronx cheer. He tells the story that you and your dad and Dennis were in an elevator and a woman walks in and recognizes Bobby's father. She says, "Aren't you Mr. Hull?" He said, "Yes, this is my son Bobby," and then pointed to Dennis and said, "And this is his brother."

There is a legendary story about Dennis that I have to share.

In the mid-'70s, there was a huge gala for charity in Los Angeles. The idea was that someone from every sport and every form of entertainment would come on stage and talk for a few minutes. It was a massive event, with the likes of Frank Sinatra and Johnny Carson coming on stage and doing a routine. Somehow, Dennis was the player who was going to represent hockey.

Just before Dennis went on, Beverly Sills, the opera singer, brought down the house with a great performance. She got a standing ovation and walked off the stage, blowing kisses. Then they introduced Dennis. He walked out on stage and stood in front of the microphone until everything settled down. He looked around and said, "I bet you thought this gala was all over." There was a murmur in the crowd. He said it again, "I bet you thought this gala was all over, right?" The crowd looked more confused. Then Dennis said, "Well, we all know it's over when the fat lady sings."

Half the audience roared with laughter and the other half gasped. Beverly Sills' people went nuts and they dragged Dennis off stage.

Not too sure how much of this is true and how much is a myth, but it is pretty funny.

* * *

After we finished the interview, Bobby stayed around to sign autographs, take pictures and tell more stories. Bobby was always great with the fans. I remember one time I was in Rochester, playing for the Amerks. The team went to see him play in Chicago. He was going for his 50th goal against Bruce Gamble. Bobby signed autographs for almost the entire warm-up, and when he was leaving the ice, he stopped and signed more autographs.

Bobby never forgot the fans.

ON COACHING

Me in action in Madison Square Garden.
That's Brad Park I'm tapping on the shoulder.

I'M STANDING IN A COLD ARENA and feeling so sad as I see
my grandson Del, who is a goalie, practise. As the practice
drags on, I see the love of hockey slowly being drawn out
of the young players' eyes.

I can remember all the good times I've had when
going on the ice and playing hockey. I can remember
doing up my skates, my hands shaking with excitement.
In Bobby Orr's book, he talks about when he was a
young lad, how he used to skate on the river near his
house. His father, Doug, would always have a hard time
getting Bobby to come into the house for supper. He used
to play by the light of the moon until it was time for

bed. He just used to play—no drills, just get the puck and go.

I don't want to knock minor coaches. They put a lot of time and effort into coaching and do a job that a lot of fathers don't want to do. But many of them are lost when it comes to how to run a practice and deal with young hockey players. And they don't get much help from Hockey Canada.

I now watch Del's practice run by well-meaning, but—I'm sorry to say—misguided coaches. I get sad looking at the kids standing around, yawning in the corner, bored stiff just doing drills. Even before the kids get on the ice, I am already getting upset. For some reason, before they get on the ice, the kids are told, "You have to remember only one out of 100,000 will ever make it to the NHL"—putting a negative thought in their heads right away, killing their dreams before they even step onto the ice. The coaches then turn it around and say it's all about fun, which it is, and then they have drill after drill, rolling around on the ice, jumping over sticks, and you can see that the kids are bored and really not having fun. I don't get that. First, they tell the kids they're not going to make the NHL, and then they do boring drills so they can get better and maybe make the NHL.

So, what should they do? you ask. Scrimmage.

Just drop the puck and let them go. Let them learn how to handle the puck, skate with the puck, just get out of their way when they are first starting and let them have fun. Every kid will tell you that scrimmaging is more fun than doing drills. The problem is that it doesn't look good to the parents, and almost all of the stuff that is done in practice is to impress the parents. I remember one time, Wayne Cashman was watching some kids jump over hurdles in a practice. A reporter asked Cash what he thought of the drill. Cash said, "When a track and field guy starts skating, then I'll think about young hockey players jumping over hurdles."

I once asked Bobby Orr's father, Doug, "How did Bobby become Bobby?" He said he really didn't know, he just let them play. That is the secret: just let the young kids play.

Bobby's parents, Doug and Arva, were great hockey parents. They encouraged Bobby to be the best he could be and never criticized him—a lesson for all hockey parents.

I want to talk about hockey parents for a minute. The media just loves to malign hockey parents. There are no better parents than hockey parents. Nobody sacrifices as much as hockey parents. They pay a ton of dough for their sons or daughters to play hockey. They drive over hell's half acre, sometimes in terrible conditions, to get to games or practices. They have to stand in cold rinks three, four, or sometimes more nights a week. No weekends off; that's when most of the games are played. The winter holidays are reserved for hockey tournaments.

Just down the road from my house is a soccer field. In the summer, games are played on Tuesday through Thursday and some games on Friday. On the weekends, the soccer fields are empty. I asked one soccer parent why the kids don't play on the weekend and he said, "Because many of the parents and players go up to the cottage on the weekend and a lot stay till Monday, so the games are Tuesday to Thursday. Over the long weekends in the summer, there are no games scheduled for the same reason."

Not hockey. Weekends are game time. Over the Christmas holiday is the busiest time for hockey tournaments. March break is playoff time. Hockey parents are 100 percent committed to their kid's passion. Most all hockey parents (there are always a few jerks in every crowd) know that their child is not going to make it to the NHL, but they see that their son or daughter loves the game and they want them to play and enjoy the sport they love.

When I hear someone say, "Oh, I won't have my child play hockey because of all the violence," to me that's code for "I don't want to spend the time and money for my kid to play hockey." I've read many an article in the newspapers about how bad hockey parents are and how foolish they are to spend so much time and money on their children's hockey. Hockey parents are easy targets for the media. I ask you this: Would someone from the media even think of going to a parent of a child who loves to play the violin and say, "Your child will never play Carnegie Hall, so why spend time and money on violin lessons for your son or daughter?" Of course not. I'll say to young violin players what I say to young hockey players: somebody has to make the NHL, somebody has to play Carnegie Hall, so why not you? Whatever your child's passion is, encourage them. I never understand people who discourage kids from trying to be the best.

Don't destroy a young person's dream. I will give you an example of how a teacher or coach can destroy dreams.

I went to school at Kingston Collegiate and Vocational Institute in Kingston, Ontario. One day a counsellor came into our classroom and said, "Only half of you will graduate from college." Well, I was in the bottom half of the class, so I wondered, "Why should I finish school if I'm not going to go to college?" He put the thought in my head, and I didn't finish school. If he had encouraged me, maybe—just maybe—things would have been different.

* * *

Every year, Hockey Canada comes out with a new book of drills for young players. I would say that this amuses me, but what it really does is burns me. I get ticked off when I see the coach stop practice, call the kids over to a board and start going over the next drill. Ice time costs a ton of dough and there the coaches are, wasting time and money going through new drills. Here is a tip: if you have a new drill, go over it with the team in the dressing room, not when you're on the ice and the meter is running at $200 an hour. Like I said, when the coach has the kids kneeling (when I coached high school hockey, the kids never knelt—I told them never to kneel before anybody), it is more a show for the parents than for the benefit of the kids.

A long time ago, I was out watching the minor midgets (15 and 16 years old) in the Greater Toronto Hockey League. At the time, the best team in the league was unbelievable during a game. They threw the puck around like the Harlem Globetrotters. Halfway through the season, I asked the coach what he did in his practices. He told me that he did a few line rushes at the start and then scrimmaged the rest of the time. After the season, every kid on that team except the backup goalie had either been drafted by a team in the Ontario Hockey League or had a college scholarship offer. I saw the coach that summer and he was down in the dumps. I congratulated him on the success of his players moving on to the next level of hockey. He said, "Grapes, they don't want me back next year." I asked him why. "Because the parents didn't like my practices. They said I should have had more drills and less scrimmage. They felt like the scrimmage was just letting the kids have fun, and anybody could do that." I wanted to cry for him. They wanted him to do drills and have the kids stand around a blackboard.

Brian Kilrea, the most successful coach in junior hockey history, who has sent more kids to the NHL than anybody, who has won two Memorial Cups, who has been junior coach of the year four times, never used a blackboard on the ice. Never in his 33 years of coaching the Ottawa 67's did he stop the practice, go over to the boards and show the team a new drill. Any new drill or anything he wanted to talk to the players about, he did it in the dressing room before they went onto the ice. Speaking of Brian, he did one thing that I would not recommend to you young coaches. Brian would stand right at centre ice when the team was doing line rushes. Players would be zipping right by him and just missing him. I asked him why he did that, and he said he liked being in the middle of the action. Well, standing at centre ice with two-on-ones and three-on-twos roaring around you will keep you in the action.

I'd go out to watch Del's practices and I'd just shake my head. One night, the coaches were explaining a drill they wanted the kids to do. It was so complicated, the Montreal Canadiens would have had a tough time understanding it. The kids couldn't get it right, so the coaches stopped the practice and started to show the kids one more time how to do the drill. I saw it coming: the coaches got a little mixed up and collided at centre ice with one another, and one coach actually broke his leg. You'd think that if the coaches can't do the drill without injuring one another, it might be a little too complicated for 10-year-olds. As the year came to a close, I asked if I could run a practice. The parents said yes, and before the team went on the ice I told the players that half the team was to wear their away sweaters and the other half their home sweaters. I went on the ice with the kids and we started with them breaking (speeding up) between the blue lines and then took some shots on the goalies to warm them up.

(That's another issue. All you young coaches, remember that goalies are not just there for target practice. Find things for them to do and include them in everything. One day when Del was about nine, he was standing in the net, doing nothing, and a coach wound up and blasted a slapshot and Del caught it and broke his finger. I wanted to strangle the guy. So, remember: goalies are not just for target practice.)

Okay, back to the practice. After warming them up, I went to centre ice and dropped the puck. They had a ball, and without them knowing it, they were working hard. Towards the end of the practice we did some drills, mostly line rushes, and then I had a special thing I wanted to do at the end of the practice. I gathered the players in the home sweaters at one end of the ice and the players in the away sweaters at the other end. I threw a puck in each end and told them to hang on to the puck and play keep away. The kids went nuts getting the puck and trying to hang on to it as the other kids tried to take it away. They had a blast and were exhausted at the end of the practice. I don't think the parents were too impressed, but the kids had fun, they handled the puck and worked hard, the way it should be at every practice. The kids came up to me and said that that practice was the most fun they had all year. Isn't that what it's all about?

I know what you're thinking: "Okay, Don, scrimmaging is fun for the kids, but what are they learning?" What they are learning during a scrimmage is something they can never learn in a drill: how to think the game. Let me guess what your son or daughter's team's breakout drill looks like. The drill starts with the coach dumping the puck behind the net and the goalie comes out and stops the puck for the defenceman. The defenceman takes two strides and passes it to a winger, who's usually standing still, and he passes it the centreman going up the middle of the ice. It looks great for the parents up in the stands, but it works about once in 100 times in a game.

When you scrimmage, the kids learn to adapt to the play. They learn what to do if an opposing player is covering the winger. The most important thing they learn—and this is very important for kids, especially teenagers—is how to play without the puck. If you think about it, for

80 percent of a game, a player doesn't have the puck on his stick. I can spot minor midget teams that don't scrimmage after watching them for two shifts. The biggest telltale sign is that the players without the puck have no clue what to do. They don't know where to go to get open for a pass. They don't know who to pick up on the back-check. They don't know what to do when the puck is in their end of the ice. They either run around and get caught out of position or stand still like deer in the head-lights. When you scrimmage, you can point out what a player should be doing when he or she doesn't have the puck. Scrimmaging also encourages the kids to learn to handle the puck in a game situation.

On that note, encourage the kids to handle the puck. I can't stand it when I'm at a minor midget game and I hear the coach and parents yell, "Pass the puck" or "The puck can move faster than you." Let the kids handle the puck, especially defencemen. If a young defenceman has the ability to carry the puck, encourage it. That's what all NHL teams are looking for: a defenceman that can carry the puck. It drives me nuts to see a young defenceman roaring up the ice with the puck, and then he knows the coach wants him to pass the puck just for the sake of passing it, and he dumps the puck to a winger standing still at the blue line. It reminds me of when I coached the IceDogs and we would play the Sault Ste. Marie Greyhounds. They had a player named Trevor Daley, who won the Cup with Sidney Crosby and the Pittsburgh Penguins in 2017, and could he motor. Every time he got the puck, he could have walked through the whole team.

He'd roar up the ice to our blue line, and then he'd stop and pass the puck. As the coach of the IceDogs, I didn't understand why he would do that, but I was awfully glad he did.

One last thing on scrimmaging: don't keep blowing the whistle when someone makes a mistake. When the player makes a mistake, tell him what he did wrong when he comes to the bench. There is nothing worse than getting a good flow going in a scrimmage and then the coach blows the whistle for some trivial reason.

Another thing for you coaches of young players: if you do have skating drills, the young hockey players should always have a puck. If you are going to make the young kids skate through pylons and things like that, make sure they have a puck. The reason is you want players to handle a puck like it's second nature. I see a lot of kids at the minor midget level that can fly without the puck, but as soon as they get it, they slow down. They should learn to handle the puck without thinking.

* * *

To be honest, when I was playing, I never thought about being a coach, but when I started, I remembered the things I didn't like as a player. Looking back at the coaches I had over 18 years of pro hockey, I learned more about what not to do than what to do as a coach. The two best coaches I had were Punch Imlach, when he coached the Springfield Indians, and Toe Blake, when I was up for a cup of coffee with the Montreal Canadiens. The one thing

I learned from Toe and the Canadiens is that you treat everybody with respect and treat them well. In the John Ferguson chapter, Fergy said that on the first day of training camp in Montreal, Toe would split the camp into four teams and then drop the puck and scrimmage.

In the 1957–58 season, Punch Imlach was the coach in Springfield and Eddie Shore was the owner. At the start of the season, Punch called me into his office to sign my contract. He gave me the contract, I signed it and he said, "Aren't you going to negotiate?"

I said, "Are you going to give me any more money?"

Punch said, "No." Then he went on to say, "You know, Don, I'm going to make the NHL one day. I think you can make the NHL too. Keep it going."

I really appreciated the encouragement, but I laughed to myself, saying, "Sure, this little bald guy is going to make it to the NHL." Sure enough, a year later he was in the NHL with the Leafs, and two years later started a three-year Stanley Cup winning streak. Punch had made the big time and I was stuck in Siberia with Shore.

A few years later, Punch came back down to Springfield to watch a game. I had been suspended by Shore for some reason or another, and I saw Punch in the hallway. He came up to me, shook my hand and said, "Hey, Donny, how are things? How is Rose doing?" Now, you may not think that was a big deal, but it meant the world to me.

I liked many things Punch did with the team, like scrimmaging, except for one major thing. As I'm writing this, during a Winnipeg Jets practice, Blake Wheeler and Ben Chiarot got into a fight and coach Paul Maurice kicked them off the ice. When two guys fought during one of Punch's practices in Springfield, he'd just let them go. I got into a fight with a teammate named Tony Schneider from Regina, Saskatchewan. Tony was a pretty tough guy and had over 100 minutes in penalties that season. I can't remember why, but we started to fight and Punch didn't let the other players break it up. We just went at it for what seemed like an hour. I can't say it was the toughest fight I was ever in, but it was the most tiring. I was so exhausted after the fight that I couldn't bend over and pick up my gloves. My hands were shaking so badly, Brian Kilrea had to pick them up and hand them to me.

Tony was skating towards the bench and must have felt something trickling down around his eye. He had a little cut, and when he saw the blood, he let out a yell that I can only describe as a cross between a Tarzan yell and Godzilla roar. He came running back, and even though I was tired, I was ready for round two. A few players got between us, and that was that until we got into the dressing room. I was taking off my elbow pads and I saw Tony coming towards me out of the corner of my eye. Again, I had to get ready for round two, but he came up and stuck out his hand and said something like "I guess I picked on the wrong guy," or something to that effect.

When I coached (and I coached the toughest teams in hockey), I would never let two guys fight in practice. Two of my favorites, Terry O'Reilly and Mike Milbury, who were good friends (if I remember correctly, they were room-mates), went at it during a practice. Even though we broke it up fairly early in the fight, there was still blood all over the glass. That is one of the main reasons I was always on the ice during a practice—because I knew I had a lot of tough guys in the club and I made sure I could control them.

* * *

When I am out at the minor midget games in Toronto, a lot of times a young guy will come up to me and ask, "How do I get into coaching?" I always tell them that they have to start in minor hockey and learn how to coach, and then work their way up to junior and then the pros. That's how I did it. When I was in Rochester, and unemployed, a man named Bob Clarke, who was the president of the Rochester Americans when I played my last few seasons, asked me to coach the Pittsford Knights high school hockey team. I agreed, but there was a problem: you had to be a teacher to be able to coach a high school sports team. So a Pittsford teacher named Joyce Sheldon was officially the coach. She took care of any off-ice stuff that needed to be dealt with, and I was the guy on the ice and on the bench.

While coaching the Knights, I learned how to run a practice and change lines. Everything that I liked in practices when I was a player, I put into my practices with the Knights. Some things worked and others didn't. I was learning how to be a coach.

The one thing I learned in my 18 years of playing pro hockey is that a team lives or dies by its special teams. The power play we had in Pittsford was the best power play I ever had. If you got a penalty against us, it was an automatic goal. First, we had a very good centreman with a ton of hockey smarts named Jay Hill. Every power play needs a guy to go into the corner and dig the puck out and battle in front of the net (back then, you stood in front of the net in any level of hockey and you got rocked), someone with the heart of a lion, and for us that was Eddie Scott. You need that guy on the blue line that has the smarts, can handle the puck and can hammer a puck. Our guy was John Hoff. He had a cannon on the point. He would let a shot go about five inches off the ice, and it always hit the net. We had guys that could handle the puck and knew what to do when they didn't have the puck—players like Al Vyverberg, Jeff Knisely and Tracy Putnam. We went undefeated in the regular season and in the playoffs, winning the championship. We had a great powerhouse team, and all we did in practice was scrimmage like Toe Blake did in his practices.

How did I get to coach in Rochester? After the undefeated season in Pittsford, I was still unemployed. Coaching high school didn't pay any money, so I made a comeback and made the Rochester Americans. I was still coaching Pittsford at the time, and about halfway through the season Doug Adam, who was coach and GM of the Amerks, quit when a fan punched him in the head after we lost 8–1 to Nova Scotia. I took over, with the team in last place, and in the end we missed the playoffs by one point, tying the last game of the season. I helped out Pittsford as much as I could that year, but the Amerks were the main focus. When I left Pittsford, we had a 6–0 record.

* * *

One last story about scrimmaging. To make a good scrimmage, you have to have two goalies who are into the practice. In Boston, we had Gerry Cheevers, and he never liked to practise. In fact, many times during an optional practice, I'd tell Gerry not to bother putting on the equipment and just go out for a skate. He'd put on a sweat suit and just skate around, taking shots at Gilles Gilbert. When we'd scrimmage, Gerry would actually get out of the way of the pucks. Terry O'Reilly, as you'll read in his chapter, was very serious and intense about practice. One day, Terry came up to me and said, "Grapes, you have to do something about Cheevers. He's ruining the scrimmages. He won't even try and stop the puck."

I knew Cheevers wasn't going to change, so I told Terry, "Okay, every time you hit Cheevers in the right pad with the puck, we'll consider that a goal." I told him not to tell Cheevers. So the next scrimmage, every time someone hit Gerry on the right pad, they celebrated like it was a goal.

After a few days of this, Gerry skated up to me and said, "Grapes, have you noticed how much better I am doing in the scrimmages?" I told him he was doing a great job. A few days later, somebody told Gerry. He didn't talk to me for a month.

So, you are asking, besides bragging, what is the point? The point is if you ever get the chance to coach, scrimmage instead of running those dull, boring drills. The kids will love it (and isn't that what it's all about?) and they will learn a lot about how to play the game.

Remember: scrimmage and you'll have a step up on everybody, and in the end, you will win.

FIGHTING

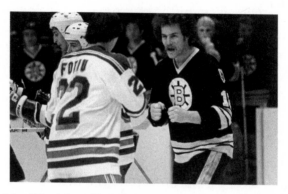

John Wensink vs. Nick Fotiu at Madison Square Garden.
The linesmen broke off the fight before anything happened and
the New York crowd went nuts.

WHEN YOU TALK ABOUT FIGHTING IN hockey, you have to
realize that it is politically incorrect to say it should be part
of the game. It's tough for me to see players who made a
good living in the NHL by fighting who are now putting
fighting down. They know that if you want to survive in
the media world, you'd better learn to say things like this
about fighting: "Well, if you like that kind of thing . . ." or
"I don't mind a spontaneous fight, but I hate the staged
fighting," or "Some people like it."

I look at the NHL today, and as I write this, Auston
Matthews of the Toronto Maple Leafs is out with an injury,
Jack Eichel of the Buffalo Sabres is out, Mark Scheifele of

the Winnipeg Jets is out, and the Boston Bruins have six guys out of the lineup.

I cannot understand how coaches and GMs let their stars take the abuse in today's game. Look at the 2017 Stanley Cup semifinal series between the Pittsburgh Penguins and the Ottawa Senators. It went seven games and Sidney Crosby only had three goals, all on the power play.

One of the main reasons the Sens were one goal away from making the Stanley Cup final was the way defence-man Marc Methot roughed up Crosby throughout the series. Marc was cross-checking, face washing and giving Crosby a hard time when they were on the ice. Now, don't get me wrong; I love Methot, and that was his job. He was doing what he had to do, and I said on "Coach's Corner" that the Sens were going to be sorry they let him go in the expansion draft. But there was no way the Penguins should have let him do that number on Crosby the way he did over those seven games. If they had an enforcer, he would have stepped up and made Methot pay for his actions.

Sid "The Kid" Crosby, the greatest player in the game today, has had a few concussions. Back in the '70s and '80s, he would have been off-limits. Whatever team he was playing for would have had an enforcer, and if you touched Crosby, you would have paid a heavy price. It would have been known throughout the league that if you hit him, checked him too closely or just bugged him, you'd have to be prepared to answer for your actions and drop the gloves. I guarantee you that if Crosby played on my Bruins, there is no way he would have had even one concussion.

Connor McDavid, the second-best player in the league today, had his collarbone broken in his rookie year. If you don't remember, he was cutting hard to the net in a game against Philly, and Flyers defencemen Brandon Manning and Michael Del Zotto took him out hard. They crashed into the boards and snapped his collarbone. When McDavid was in a vulnerable position, the Flyers showed no mercy and drove him into the boards.

I went on "Coach's Corner" and said, "Ladies and gentlemen, I am steaming. I've been waiting for this 'Coach's Corner' to show dummies like you [I pointed to Ron] that Connor McDavid was hurt on purpose. You're going to say, 'Oh, well, it's just a hockey play.' I'm telling you they meant to drive him into the boards."

Boy, did I get roasted in the paper. Everybody was calling me a dinosaur, the usual stuff. After a rough game with Philly a year later, McDavid said in the paper, "I did all I could defending him last year in the media. Everyone wanted to make a big deal, saying he did it on purpose, and he wanted to say some comments today about what went on last year. I thought it was one of the [most] classless things I've ever seen on the ice. He said some things and our guys responded accordingly. I guess we can put the whole 'if he did it on purpose' thing to rest, because what he said out there kind of confirmed that. Shows what kind of guy he is when he doesn't step up and fight some of our guys."

I don't like saying "I told you so," but I told you so. There was no doubt in my mind that those two guys meant to hurt him. Now, I'm not saying they meant to break his shoulder, but they showed no mercy. If those guys did that to Detroit's Steve Yzerman in the '80s, they would have had to face Bob Probert and Joey Kocur when it was all said and done. Again, if McDavid played for my Bruins, there is no way that would have happened. If it did, the game would still be going on, as we would deal out our revenge on those two players.

* * *

A classic example of how fighting can protect a star is Jean Ratelle. When Jean came to the Bruins, he had a bad back. It was so bad that when we went on the road, we had to get a board put under his mattress to help ease his back pain. When you saw him walk in his street clothes, he walked very upright—like most people with bad backs. When he was with the Rangers, Jean was Mr. New York. In fact, the Rangers retired Jean's number 19 just this year. The reason the Rangers traded Jean to us in 1975 was because they thought his career was finished. I remember after the trade, there was a cartoon in the paper showing Rangers GM Emile Francis with a bandit's mask on, creeping away with Phil Esposito and Carol Vadnais, and Bruins GM Harry Sinden looking sad with Brad Park with a bad knee and Jean with a bad back.

Little did everyone know that the trade was the best thing for Jean's career. We protected our stars in Boston, and the Rangers didn't. Jean had a resurgence in his career and went on to play six more years. I had Jean for three full seasons from 1976–77 to 1978–79 and he missed a total of two games (he got the flu) out of 240. It was known throughout the league if you touched or messed with Jean—or any of our smaller players—you would have to face O'Reilly, Wensink, Jonathan, Secord or Cashman. Just like if we bothered the Islanders' Mike Bossy, we'd have to face Clark Gillies, Bryan Trottier, Garry Howatt, Gerry Hart or Bob Nystrom. That was the law of the jungle.

Today, it's open season on the stars—or anyone for that matter. You don't have to pay the price for your actions. Look how they run the goalies now. People keep asking why there is so much goalie interference; I'll tell you why: guys that run the goalies don't have to pay a price. There are a lot of cheap shots taken today that would never be thought of in the past. Before he had to become politically correct as the GM in Tampa, Steve Yzerman said he'd rather see two guys drop the gloves than little rats with visors running around sticking guys.

I was watching the game between the Penguins and the Bruins on March 7, 2010. The Bruins' Marc Savard, one of my favourites, took a pass from Milan Lucic just inside the Penguins' blue line and took a shot on net. The Penguins' Matt Cooke was in Savard's blind spot and just levelled him. Savard didn't have a chance; he was KO'd and was taken off on a stretcher, and that pretty much ended Marc's career. It was one of the dirtiest hits I've seen. And nothing happened. The Bruins didn't go after Cooke, and in the end the NHL didn't suspend him.

I was just steaming. I went on "Coach's Corner" the next Saturday and said, "The hit on Savard by Cooke, call it what you want, a cheap shot, blindside hit or whatever, but I cannot believe it was not a suspension. . . . It's a funny thing that Cooke never, ever hits the tough guys. He hits guys like [Vincent] Lecavalier or [Erik] Cole or Marc or guys like that. . . . This guy deliberately tries to hurt people. You think he'd try this stuff on Gretzky when Semenko was there? Do you think he'd do these things to Yzerman if Probert was there? No. That's what I've been trying to tell you.

"I am going to tell you a story about this guy. Remember that cheap shot against Cole in Carolina in the playoffs last year? After the game, I met him in the hall—or he met me in the hall—and he said to me, 'Are you going to have the guts to say to my face what you say on TV?' I was about six inches from his face and said, 'You're a gutless, backstabbing little—' I can't say what I called him."

Cooke and I did go at it in the hall, and not too long ago I saw a video of it on YouTube.

For guys like Matt Cooke, the instigator rule took out any fear of having to pay the price. Back in the '70s and '80s, the enforcer and the fear of having to physically pay a price for your actions would have stopped guys like Cooke and other cheap-shot artists from blindsiding guys like Savard. Matt got suspended a few times later in his career and I must admit he played the game the way it should be played—mean but fair—at the end of his career.

* * *

The biggest reason today's stars are not protected is the instigator rule. It was brought in when Gil Stein was running the NHL in 1992. The rule stated if you started the fight, you'd get an extra two minutes, along with a five-minute major and a 10-minute misconduct. So if someone came to Crosby's aid when Methot was doing his number on him, they would have gotten 17 minutes in penalties. If someone from Boston went after Cooke after his hit on Savard and Cooke turtled, the Bruins would have had to kill a seven-minute power play.

The NHL Board of Governors were worried at the time that the enforcers were going to start to get into fights with the stars. Very rarely did an enforcer get into a fight with a star that couldn't fight, but one morning the board of governors woke up and started worrying about that situation. A lot of hockey people started saying that this rule was going to cause a lot of problems on the ice. So the next thing the governors wanted us to believe was that the instigator rule would crack down on fighting, and the less fighting there was, the more Americans would like hockey. When I first heard someone say that on the air, I thought they were joking, but unfortunately they weren't. Right . . . American fans don't like fights. Are they crazy? I played all over the United States, and when there was a save, they'd give a little cheer; when there was a hit, they'd give a little bigger cheer; when there was a goal, they'd give a little bigger cheer; but when there was a fight, they'd go nuts. When I was coaching Colorado and the Stanley Cup champs came in, we'd get around 12,000 fans; when the Broad Street Bullies came to town, it was a complete sellout, with another 2,000 fans waiting to get inside. To say American fans don't like fights is nuts.

The NHL can never take out the instigator rule. Once you put something like that in, it's impossible to reverse.

If the NHL said that the instigator rule was gone, they would get crucified in the press. The media would say the league wants more violence and that vigilante justice is barbaric. The fans would like it, the players would like it, the superstars would like it, but the press would go bananas and the NHL can't go to war with the press, so the instigator rule is here to stay.

The other thing that changed was the role of the enforcer. When I was coaching the Bruins, all my tough guys played. In the 1977–78 season, Terry O'Reilly led the team in points and in penalty minutes. That season, the three tough guys on my Bruins—O'Reilly, Stan Jonathan and John Wensink—had a combined total of 178 points and 500 minutes in penalties, with 35 fights. Al Secord went on to score 50 goals. They all played regular. Same with the Flyers. Schultz and their tough guys, they all played regular. You can say the same about the New York Islanders and the Montreal Canadiens. When the Oilers had Dave Semenko, who was there to make sure no one fooled with Wayne Gretzky, he played fairly regular and when Marty McSorley came to Edmonton to take over Semenko's role, he played regular.

Then the enforcers started to become mad dogs. They'd sit on the bench and just wait to get out and fight. I can't stand that, and I'd never do that on my team. If you can't play regular, you shouldn't be on the team. These enforcers who are treated like mad dogs got into a Catch-22 situation. If a tough guy sits on the bench and gets one or two shifts a game, he has to start something. If he doesn't fight, then people say, "Why is he on the team?" So he has to go out and fight, and then people say, "He only plays a little and all he does is fight." He loses both ways.

Fortunately, it has changed. Now, you must be able to play the game. No team now has a guy on the bench who just fights. Take a look at the two toughest guys in this year's Stanley Cup finals. Ryan Reaves and Tom Wilson can both play the game and are tough as nails.

* * *

Every year, the fighting seems to go down in the NHL and the injuries to the star players go up. The "experts" tell me that it's just a coincidence. I always tell them that if the number of fights went up and the number of injuries to the stars went up, they'd be saying it was because of the fighting. Once fighting is out of the game, it will never come back. Then watch the injuries.

FRED SHERO

Two-time Stanley Cup winner Fred Shero. Fred was way ahead of his time.

A STUDENT OF THE GAME

EVERYBODY KNOWS THAT THE BRUINS' biggest rival is Montreal, but a close second would be the Philadelphia Flyers. When I started with the Bruins, the Broad Street Bullies were in full swing and their coach was Freddy "The Fog" Shero. Fred was born in Winnipeg and played for the New York Rangers for three years. He retired from playing in 1958 and started following his true calling, coaching. Fred honed his craft for 13 years in the minors before he made it to the NHL as coach of the Flyers in 1971. That first season, they didn't make the playoffs, but the next year the Broad Street Bullies were born, and in his third year they won the Stanley Cup.

Fred was a real student of the game.

We interviewed Fred in 1982, when he had gone from coaching to the broadcast booth. Fred was starting as the colour man for the New Jersey Devils, who had just moved from Colorado. Now, most everybody knew that the Devils and the Pittsburgh Penguins were in a race to the bottom to see who would get the first pick overall and win the Mario Lemieux sweepstakes.

DON: I heard you're going to be colour man for the New Jersey Devils broadcast.

FRED: Yes, I did my first broadcast last week. I will say, it is much easier than coaching. You don't have to worry if you win or lose. Don't sweat at all. You get into the game for nothing.

DON: That's for sure. Now, you are a real student of the game. You went over to Russia to study the game. You paid your own way over to Finland to learn how they play the game. I got to ask: Why weren't you asked ever to coach Team Canada in any international tournaments?

FRED: Maybe they don't know my phone number. I have actually studied the Russians since 1947—that's when they started playing hockey. The reason I went to Finland was to learn how they play hockey. I still might accept a job coaching in Europe or Asia. Especially China. China has gone crazy over hockey. I'd like to do a study of every country that plays hockey and find out why they do things differently than we do. I want to find out why they think they do things better than we do. Is it their lifestyle or what? Then I want to write a book on the subject.

It seems like Fred was way ahead of his time. Of course, now the NHL wants to get into China and had its first exhibition games there a few years ago. I guess hockey is growing in China, just like Fred said it was going to. My granddaughter Grace spent a month in China a few years ago and said she saw rinks in shopping malls and kids were playing.

NO MAD DOGS

FOR ALL THOSE WHO DON'T KNOW the history of the Broad Street Bullies, they took Conn Smythe's slogan—"If you can't beat 'em in the alley, you can't beat 'em on the ice"—to a whole new level. In 1974, the Flyers basically beat up the entire NHL along the road to becoming the first expansion team to win the Stanley Cup. The Flyers went on to repeat the next year with the same tactic. Their motto was "The ref can't call everything."

When they first won the Cup in 1974, the team racked up over 1,700 minutes in penalties. To give you some perspective, in 2016–17, Ottawa's Mark Borowiecki led the NHL with 154 minutes in penalties. In 1974, Dave "The Hammer" Schultz led the Flyers with 348 penalty minutes, including 18 majors. The next year, when Philadelphia won the Cup again, they had even more penalties—over 1,950 penalty minutes, with "The Hammer" racking up a record 472 minutes in penalties, including 25 majors, with the team dropping the gloves a total of 92 times. When teams would play the Flyers at the Spectrum (located at 3501 South Broad Street in Philadelphia, hence the nickname Broad Street Bullies), players would get the "Philly Flu" and claim that they couldn't play that game.

Fred made no apologies for his team's play.

The season before our 1982 interview with Fred, there was a really bad incident in a game between LA and Vancouver. It was January 24, 1982, and there was a line brawl going on. The Canucks' Tiger Williams was giving it to a King pretty good. The Kings' coach at the time, Don Perry, told a Kings player named Paul Mulvey, who was on the bench, "Go out there and don't dance." Mulvey didn't go, and Perry told him again to go out and "don't dance." Mulvey still didn't jump over the boards. I guess the brawl on the ice started going LA's way, and one of the Canuck players jumped over and both benches eventually emptied, but the fighting had stopped. Perry was upset that Mulvey didn't go when he was told, and the next day, Mulvey was put on waivers and sent to New Haven of the American Hockey League. When this incident got out in the press, the NHL gave Perry a 15-game suspension for telling his player to go out and fight.

> **DON:** Now, we have all heard about the thing with Perry and Mulvey. Did you ever send out Schultz or any of those guys to go at Lafleur or anybody? Now,

let's face it, Fred, they did go out and do a pretty good number on teams.

FRED: I'll tell you the truth: never in my life have I asked a man to fight. The first words I say in training camp are, "If I ask you to fight, break that stick right over my head." I have no right to ask you to fight. I never once asked Schultz to fight, and my biggest job was to try and stop him from fighting so much. In his book, he said I never told him to fight. I coached Reggie Fleming, and he was even worse than Schultz, and I never told him to fight. There are certain people who are abrasive by nature. They are born that way and you're not going to change them. And when they finish hockey, they are still going to be in trouble later in life. They can do well in life, but they are going to run into various troubles because of their nature. But I still believe, and you had some abrasive guys, if you want a winner, you have to have four or five abrasive people. The Montreal Canadiens were tough for years. They didn't fight much, but they didn't have to because they had the toughest guys in hockey.

The one thing that Fred and I had in common as coaches was that we played our tough guys. We didn't have mad dogs sitting on the bench that only went out to fight. When the Flyers first won the Cup in '74, Schultz had 20 goals and 36 points and was a plus-26 to go with his 348 minutes in penalties. All my tough guys in Boston played and scored—that's why we set an NHL record of eleven 20-goal scorers. I could never have a guy sit on the bench and just go out and fight.

It happened to me once when I was a player. I was playing for Rochester, and we were in Quebec City. I had not played a shift all game, and it was late in the third. A tough defenceman named Bryan Watson from Bancroft, Ontario, was really giving our players a rough time in front of Quebec's net. Late in the game, the faceoff was in Quebec's end and my coach, Joe Crozier, told me to go and play wing. Now, I was a defenceman and never played wing in my life. Crozier never told me to fight, but I knew what he wanted me to do. Like Freddy said, "There are certain people who are abrasive by nature. They are born that way and you're not going to change them."

Right off the faceoff, Watson crosschecked me and we got into a real beauty. Ended up in a bench-clearing brawl to end all bench-clearing brawls. After the game, Joe gave me $100—he said it was a Christmas bonus. I took the money and bought $50 worth of Christmas gifts for Tim and Cindy and bought a bunch of rounds for the guys with the rest.

THEY'RE GOING HOME

AFTER THE '72 SERIES AND THE 1976 Canada Cup, someone figured out there was money to be made by having NHL teams play the Red Army and Soviet Wings teams during the middle of the NHL season. When I coached Boston, we played the Russians twice.

The second time we played them was in 1979, and I remember that game like it was yesterday. Not because we played the Russians in the middle of the season, but because it was the night they retired Bobby Orr's number 4 sweater. The fans were getting a little bored of the Russians coming over and playing NHL players. There was the '72 series, the '74 series between Russia and the WHA, the '76 Canada Cup, the '75–76 Super Series, the '77–78 Super Series and the Czechs came over in '77–78 to play NHL teams. Czech and Russian teams also played WHA teams in '76–77 and '77–78. It was complete overkill and the fans were getting turned off.

So when tickets went on sale for our game against the Russians, the sales were slow. Then it was announced that the Bruins were going to retire Bobby's number. I was furious. It would have been great to retire Bobby's number with Montreal or Toronto in the building, but they held this historic moment during a nothing game against the Russians, in my opinion, to sell out the building. Of course, the tickets sold out in minutes.

It was January 9, 1979, and when Bobby walked out onto the ice, the place went nuts. There was a 10-minute standing ovation. The old Boston Garden's walls were shaking. When some of the people started to give speeches, including Senator Ted Kennedy, the Bruins fans would drown them out with chants of "Bobby, Bobby." When Bobby finally spoke, he was booed when he said he was going to make a "short" speech. They would have loved to hear Bobby talk all night. I heard through the grapevine that Bobby wanted all the proceeds for the night to go to four charities in the Boston area, including Boston Children's Hospital.

So, after that emotional event, we had to play an exhibition game against the Soviet Wings. I could have cared less. We lost 4–1, thanks largely to referee Wally Harris, who gave us 55 minutes in penalties. When the press asked me about the Wings' power play, I said, "I'll give them credit for this: they can really handle the puck on the power play. Then again, they had a lot of practice on the power play tonight." When the press pushed me about how important this game was, I replied, "After Bobby Orr, it was anticlimatic. I spent the whole night watching the result of the Buffalo-Atlanta game."

It was the middle of the season and we were in a dog-fight for first place with Buffalo. We were on a roll going into the stupid game. In the 24 games leading up to it, our record was 19 wins, two losses and three ties. We were in a real groove. But all you coaches know that something like this type of nothing game can throw a team out of its rhythm. And boy, did we go off the rails. In the next 20 games, we went into the tank. Our record was seven wins, 10 losses and three ties. We lost only 23 games all season, and close to half were in the stretch right after that exhibition game. We still finished first in the Adams Division and were second only to Montreal in the league for points.

* * *

The first time we played the Russians when I coached was back in January 1976. This time, there was more interest in the game. The story line for the press was how their club teams would match up with NHL club teams. Well, first off, the Russians sent two all-star teams—they were not just regular club teams. We were going to play the Red Army, which was the stronger of the two teams. We lost 4–1, but kept with them most of the game. But, again, it was the middle of the season and the biggest thing for me was that none of our players got hurt.

The star of the game was the Red Army's goalie, Vladislav Tretiak. He was not only the star of this game, but of the whole series. We had 19 shots in the first period and 13 in the third and outshot them 41–19 for the whole game. That was the same year the Red Army played the Montreal Canadiens on New Year's Eve, and again Tretiak was the star. The Canadiens were all over them, and the only reason it ended up a 3–3 tie was Tretiak, who stopped 38 shots to only 13 fired at Dryden.

The big game was the Flyers playing the Red Army. It was their best against the Stanley Cup champions. The Broad Street Bullies had a lot of pride, and this game would mean a lot to the NHL and to Fred Shero. If the Russians beat the Stanley Cup champs, they would have beaten our best.

DON: Remember that great game in '76 when you beat the Russians? What was your game plan going into that game?

FRED: We knew it was the biggest game of our lives. We were told it was the biggest audience in sports, because 350 million people watched that game on television from all over the world. We had to win. We practised specifically for them for three weeks, sometimes twice a day. Maybe that's why we lost the Stanley Cup—it took so much out of us and it was so emotional. This was our game plan: never shoot unless to score. I mean, if you had a clear shot. Yet we had 43 good shots on them. When we had the puck in their end, [we didn't] worry about getting hit.

DON: Because they won't hit you.

FRED: That's right. Just hold it or freeze it, because we were going to win the draw anyway. They were terrible on the draws. So we controlled the puck more than they did. When they started this silly nonsense of zigzagging and circling in their zone, we just held our ground. They have to come to us, so they made 20 passes in the zone and we wouldn't move. We'd line up five men along their blue line and they couldn't proceed.

Fred had a good system in place, and the Russians didn't know what they were in for, walking into the lion's den. And they made things worse by antagonizing the Flyers before the game. First, they were giving Flyers owner Ed Snider a hard time when they were negotiating the terms for them to come over and play the NHL teams. Then, a few days before the game, there was a press luncheon with both teams. The Flyers were on time and the Russians showed up late. Bobby Clarke was quoted as saying, "We were waiting for them, looking like fools." The Flyers organization got gifts for each Russian player and coach; the Russians said they didn't want them. The Russian players complained that they only had one stick each, so the Flyer players gave them some sticks. The Russian said the Flyers' sticks were no good and they didn't want them. When Brian McFarlane of *Hockey Night in Canada* asked Clarke in an interview between the first and second period the difference between playing the touring Russian team and the Montreal Canadiens or Boston Bruins, Clarke responded, "Well, both those teams have a little class."

Fred had a good plan for the Russians, but he also had the Broad Street Bullies chomping at the bit. They were the defending Stanley Cup champs and the Russians had antagonized them, so the Flyers were more than ready. The game was scoreless in the first, and Eddie Van Impe, who was as vicious as they come, was sitting in the penalty box. The Russians were coming up the ice, and right at the Flyers blue line, André "The Moose" Dupont nailed one of the Russians and he crumpled to the ice. The puck went down the ice, and when the Russian defenceman touched the puck, Billy Barber really nailed him into the boards with a clean check. The puck went up along the boards and Barber sent a Russian winger flying with another clean check. You could start to see that the Russians weren't too anxious to touch the puck.

About 10 seconds later, Eddie came out of the penalty box as Valeri Kharlamov was carrying the puck down the

ice into the Flyers end. Ed made a beeline for him and
drilled him pretty good. Now, it was a borderline hit, and
the ref didn't call a penalty. Believe me, there were a lot
more vicious hits when the Bruins and Flyers played that
didn't result in a penalty. Kharlamov lay on the ice as if he
was shot. The Russian bench was going nuts and was com-
plaining. The ref, Lloyd Gilmour from Cumberland, B.C.,
told the Russians to get on the ice or they were getting a
delay-of-game penalty. They kept on yapping, so Gilmour
followed through and gave them a bench minor. When
they announced the penalty, the fans went nuts. The
famous Philly sign man held up signs saying CHICKEN
and TELL IT TO THE CZAR. That was it. The Russians left.
They went back to the dressing room.

Bob Cole was doing the play-by-play, and when they
started to leave, Bob gave his famous call: "They're leaving.
They're going home. They're going home. Yeah, they're
going home. Can you believe it? In '72, in Moscow, we
stayed and we took it all. Now the Flyers run around a
little bit and they're going home."

In the hallway outside the Russian dressing room, Alan
Eagleson and Flyers owner Ed Snider got into it with the
Russian officials. Eagleson and Snider told them, "If you
don't play, you're not getting paid." The Russians wanted
the delay-of-game penalty cancelled. I can imagine what
Eagleson said to them about that. So they came back on
the ice after about 15 minutes or so. When the game
started up again, the Flyers scored two quick goals and
went on to win 4-1, outshooting the Russians 43-13. The
Flyers pounded them on the scoreboard, the shots on net,

and on the ice. The Russians soon learned what the "Philly Flu" was like.

HOW TO BEAT PYRAMID POWER

IN THE 1976 PLAYOFFS, FRED SHERO and the Flyers met the Toronto Maple Leafs, coached by Red Kelly. The Leafs had beaten the Penguins in the first round and had a secret weapon to help them beat the Flyers. It was "pyramid power."

> **DON:** Now, tell us about Red Kelly's pyramid power and how you beat the Leafs that year.

> **FRED:** Pyramid power almost destroyed us till I went to see a famous faith healer in Philadelphia, and she said she'd put the hex on the pyramid power. So she hovered over the pyramid for 15 minutes. I knew we were going to win, we were going to beat the Leafs.

> **DON:** Now, Kate Smith, was she on the payroll?

> **FRED:** Yes, she was. But I didn't pay her. I couldn't afford her. She was getting $10,000 a game.

> **DON:** Really? Ten grand a game? Was she worth it?

> **FRED:** Every penny. She won us two Stanley Cups.

Fred was having some fun with the audience. But both teams did have their good luck charms in that '76 series. Whenever the Flyers felt they needed a big win at home, they would bring in Kate Smith, a big star in radio and television who was known as the First Lady of Radio, to sing "God Bless America."

It started one day in 1969, when the Flyers played a recording of Kate singing "God Bless America" instead of "The Star-Spangled Banner" before a game, and they won. They soon found out that, nearly every time they played Kate's version of "God Bless America," they won. And a superstition was born.

Red Kelly developed pyramid power to help the Leafs that series. The story goes that Red's daughter Casey had a bad headache. Red's wife read somewhere that if you put a pyramid under a pillow, it would get rid of a headache. So they tried it, and it worked. Red's wife suggested that pyramids might help the team. So Red thought he'd give it a try.

The first two games in Philly, they played Kate's record of "God Bless America" and the Flyers won both games, outscoring the Leafs 7–2 in total. The next two games, back in Toronto, Red put five small pyramids under the Leafs bench. The Leafs won 5–4 in a fight-filled game. The players didn't know about the pyramids, and Red didn't tell them. They won the next game 4–3, tying the series at two.

Now it was a best-two-out-of-three series and the teams were heading back to Philly. Kate belted out "God Bless America" and the Flyers hammered the Leafs 7–1. Before

Game 6 at the Gardens, Red Kelly went public with his pyramid power and had a large pyramid hanging in the middle of the Leafs dressing room. Darryl Sittler, who had not scored a goal all playoffs, took his sticks and put them under the pyramid, and then he stood under it himself. That night, the Leafs won 8–5, and Sittler tied an NHL playoff record with five goals in one playoff game.

So, Game 7 in Philly. Red brings the pyramid to Philly and hangs it in the dressing room again. And the Flyers unleash Kate Smith. Kate overpowered the pyramids. Flyers won 7–3.

* * *

Fred won the Jack Adams Award as coach of the year for the 1973–74 season, the first year it was given out. He would fit perfectly in today's game. I think he was way ahead of his time. One of his most famous quotes, when the Flyers were up 3–2 and playing Game 6 against Boston in the '74 Stanley Cup final, was "Win today, and we walk together forever."

Good hockey genes must run in his family. I know that he would be very proud of his son Ray Shero, who won a Stanley Cup in 2009 as the GM of the Pittsburgh Penguins.

HALL OF FAME

[Inscription: To my coaching idol, Don Cherry.
All the best, your friend, Pat Burns]

I said it before and I'll say it again. Pat not going in
the Hall of Fame before he died was inexcusable.

MANY TIMES, I HAVE BEEN INTERVIEWED and asked about
the Hockey Hall of Fame. I usually just give a nothing
answer. Why would I want to say how I feel and get caught
up in the controversy of who should be in and who should
be out of the Hall of Fame? I feel strongly about some of
the people they have left out. Like I said in my last book,
how in the world did they leave out Pat Burns when he was
sick and then vote him in a few years after he died? I've
said before that his coaching record didn't improve after
he died. I vowed that he'd be in the opening of all my
"Coach's Corners," and I have a picture of him and me

with the Jack Adams Trophy when Pat won it while coaching the Boston Bruins.

Now, I want to tell you a story about Bill "Flash" Hollett. Flash was born in North Sydney, Nova Scotia, in April of 1911 but lived most of his young life in the Toronto area. When Flash was young, he played hockey as well as lacrosse. He was an excellent lacrosse player. Legend has it he was playing lacrosse with the great Lionel Conacher. One day, Toronto Maple Leafs owner and GM Conn Smythe reportedly told him, "If you can play hockey like you play lacrosse, we can use you in our organization."

Flash accepted Smythe's offer and started his pro career in the International League, playing for the Syracuse Stars. After stints in the IHL, as well as with the Ottawa Senators and Leafs, Toronto sold him to the Bruins for $16,000, and in Boston his career took off. Flash was kind of overshadowed by some of the other great defencemen on the Bruins—he was paired with Eddie Shore. Throughout the years in Boston, he started to put a lot of points on the board. He got the nickname Flash because he was such a good skater. When the Bruins were down a forward, they would move Flash up front because he could skate so well. He would also play up front when the Bruins were killing a penalty. In 1939, the Bruins and Leafs met for the Stanley Cup. Flash would score the Cup-clinching goal against the Leafs.

In 1941–42, he set an NHL record for defencemen, scoring 19 goals. Flash didn't get much respect back then either. There was no Norris Trophy, and Earl Seibert of Chicago and Tommy "Cowboy" Anderson of the Brooklyn

Americans were named as the top two defencemen. Earl scored seven goals and Cowboy scored 12 goals that season. He didn't make the Second All-Star Team either. Pat Egan of the Americans (eight goals) and Bucko McDonald of the Leafs (two goals) were considered the #3 and #4 defencemen that season. In 1942–43, Flash tied his record of 19 goals and broke Cowboy Anderson's NHL record of 44 points. That year, he made the Second All-Star Team.

Flash and Art Ross, the GM of the Bruins, clashed, and rumour has it that Ross was thinking of burying Flash in the minors, which happened more often than you'd think back then. Ross traded Flash to the Detroit Red Wings in January 1944, and the next season, he scored 20 goals and 41 points. That was in only 50 games. In 1945–46, Flash had a bad knee and only scored four goals in 38 games. Then he and the Wings' GM, Jack Adams, got into a disagreement over a $500 raise. Adams refused to give it to him, so Flash retired. He went on to play in the Ontario Hockey Association senior league and won the Allan Cup in 1950.

So when Flash retired, he had the NHL record for goals in one season by a defenceman, with 20. That record lasted for 24 years until the greatest player in history, Bobby Orr, scored 21 in 1968–69. Flash was also the highest-scoring defenceman in league history when he retired. He won two Stanley Cups with Boston, in 1939 and 1941.

So, why isn't he in the Hall of Fame? Well, I think early on it was because he butted heads with Art Ross and Jack Adams. Those guys didn't forget, and I'm betting they didn't want Flash in the Hall. But today, the Hall should look back, accept that there was an oversight and put Flash where he belongs, in the Hall of Fame. But I'm not holding my breath.

* * *

We won't go into Paul Henderson. I know I went through this in my last book, but I just want to say it again. Paul gets the winner in Game 6, Game 7 and the big one in Game 8 of the '72 Series. The Game 8 goal is the most historic goal in hockey. Paul had 10 points in eight games, three game-winning goals, and was the biggest plus—plus-10—on Team Canada. And he's not in the Hall of Fame. The Russian goalie, Vladislav Tretiak, who choked in his own country in three straight games, is in the Hall. Again, it makes you shake your head.

* * *

Another guy I can't understand not being in the Hall of Fame is Ricky Middleton. I coached Rick for three years in Boston. Everybody thinks his nickname was Nifty because he was so nifty with the puck, and he was nifty. Few players have ever been better one on one than Rick. But his real nickname was Eddie, because he looked like Eddie Munster, the character from the television series *The Munsters*.

First, I'll give you the stats. He scored 448 goals and 988 points in just over 1,000 NHL games. Then you look at his stats when they really count: in the playoffs. In 114 playoff games, Rick scored 35 goals and had 100 points, almost a point-a-game playoff performer. That includes eight game winners. In the 1981–82 season, Rick scored 51 goals and won the Lady Byng Trophy.

If I asked you who has the most points in one playoff series, you'd think of Wayne Gretzky, Mario Lemieux or Sidney Crosby. But it was Ricky Middleton. In the 1983 Adams Division final between Boston and Buffalo, Rick had 19 points—five goals and 14 assists—in seven games. A record that still stands today. Those 14 assists are also an NHL record for the most in one playoff series. That year, Rick had 33 playoff points, but the Bruins didn't make the finals. And those 33 points are the most scored by a player whose team didn't make it to the finals.

Rick played for Team Canada in the Canada Cup in 1981 and 1984. In the 1984 Canada Cup, Rick played with Gretzky and Michel Goulet and had eight points in seven games. Rick also played in three NHL All-Star Games. For him not to be in the Hall of Fame makes you wonder. There is no good reason for it. The voters had better smarten up.

DAVE SCHULTZ

Dave "The Hammer" Schultz, head of the Broad Street
Bullies and Philly fan favourite.

THE FIRST TIME I SAW DAVE "The Hammer" Schultz was
when I was playing for the Rochester Americans in my
comeback year in 1971–72. Dave was in his third year in
the American Hockey League, and he was playing for the
Richmond Robins.

I can tell you, going into Richmond was no fun. The
Richmond Coliseum would start to shake when they
played Bobby Day's "Rockin' Robin." Now, the Robins
didn't have that great a club—they were well below .500
and they missed the playoffs—but they were tough. Even
though they weren't winning a ton of games, they had the
second-highest attendance in the league.

When I took over the Rochester Americans, I kind of took a page out of the Robins' playbook and got the toughest team I could get, and Bob "Battleship" Kelly would be my Hammer. In my first year in as coach and GM in Rochester, we had the third-highest attendance in the AHL. The next year, we were basically tied for the best attendance in the league.

Richmond was the farm club of the Philadelphia Flyers, and you could see the signs of what would become the Broad Street Bullies. They had Schultz, Don Saleski, Rick MacLeish, and Bill Clement, all of whom would eventually make the NHL and win two Stanley Cups with the Flyers. And the baddest of the Broad Street Bullies was Schultz. In his first NHL season, he spent 259 minutes in the penalty box and fought 21 times. The next season, he got 348 minutes in penalties and 27 majors—he also scored 20 goals and won a Stanley Cup. The season after *that*, he set a record with 472 penalty minutes (it still stands), including 33 majors, and still found time to score 26 points and win another Stanley Cup. The fans in Philly loved the Flyers, especially their main weapon, the Hammer.

One day, Ron MacLean and I were having a few pops after a game and he asked me what I missed most about my playing days. I had to be honest, and I know it sounds terrible, but I missed the fighting. I liked to fight. The adrenaline rush you get when you know you're about to have a go is like nothing else in the world, and I do miss it to this very day.

DON: Do you remember when I played against you in Richmond?

DAVE: I remember you. I saw your name in the lineup, but your coach never put you on the ice when I was out there.

DON: I remember after a whistle, you pushed me around in the corner a bit and I pushed you back. . . . You guys sold out the arena in Richmond, and when you went to Philly, you guys sold out everywhere you went. Everybody wanted to see you guys in action. Now, I know you don't like to talk about fighting, but I'm going to ask you because it's my show. Now, I know a guy like Stan Jonathan, he liked to fight, and Terry O'Reilly, he really didn't like to fight. Now I'm going to ask you: Did you like to fight?

DAVE: Not really. But I enjoyed the rewards. The anticipation of the fights was nerve-racking. Particularly after I got a reputation. I had a reputation in the American League, of course—Fred Shero knew what I was doing down there. I soon showed him when a certain situation happened, I would be out there, doing my thing. It was that anticipation of knowing that most of the people in the stands, plus my teammates, knew that if something happened on the ice, I was the guy—we had a few others on our team—but I probably was the guy that was going to do something. When you have a reputation like that, it's not that I was worried about getting hurt physically, but I didn't want to lose in front of my fans and my teammates.

DON: I do relate to you. I played till I was 36 years old, and up until I was about 32, that is what I had to do. I had to go out if something happened on the ice and straighten it out. You're exactly right—I couldn't put in words as well as you just did—you weren't afraid of getting cut or getting hurt, you didn't want to lose in front of your teammates. Did Fred Shero ever send you out after someone?

DAVE: Well, when he heard the Boston coach was sending guys out . . .

Of course, Dave was just kidding.

DAVE: He never, ever said during a particular time in a game, "Dave, go get that guy." But when I knew it wasn't my turn to go on the ice and I found myself on the ice—or after something happened on the ice—I knew what I was to do. But to be fair, I already showed him that I was ready to do that.

DON: You guys were really on a roll in Philly. The fans loved you guys and they had the fans with the army helmets called Schultz's army, Kate Smith, the whole Broad Street Bullies—it was colourful. Boy, it must have been a lot of fun.

DAVE: It really was exciting at the time. The city of
Philadelphia was a city of losers before we started
to win. The city was starving for a championship in
anything. We were criticized all over the country,
we had a rivalry with New York and Boston. It
couldn't have been written any better than it turned
out. The parade after we won the two Cups was—
you know, I wish I would have appreciated it more
at the time, things happen so fast.

I've said many times when I was in Boston and Montreal
came to town, there would be excitement in the Garden.
When Philly came to town, the Garden was electric too.
In my five years in Boston, we met the Flyers three times
in the playoffs, so we built up a big rivalry. We had exhibition games with the Flyers that ended up in street brawls.
In my last book, I talked about the exhibition game where
author George Plimpton played goal for five minutes, and
that game had three bench-clearing brawls and there was
even fighting in the halls. Rookie-camp games between
the Flyers and the Bruins were even worse. I remember
in 1978, we had a rookie-camp game in some little rink in
Vermont. Al Secord got into three fights in that game,
and the Flyers' Ken Linseman was in the middle of
things. Of course Al made the Bruins that year.

When the Flyers and Bruins met, you knew Terry "The
Tasmanian Devil" O'Reilly and Dave "The Hammer"
Schultz were going to go. When those two were on the ice
together, there was the same feeling of anticipation as
you'd feel before a heavyweight fight.

DON: I remember when I was with the Bruins and we had Stan Jonathan come up from the minors and John Wensink came up from the minors, and they could hardly wait till they played you guys in Philly. You were the top gunfighter and they were just waiting to have a go with you. That was just two on our club. It must have been tough going into every city like that.

DAVE: Boston was the worst. You already had O'Reilly, then you had to come with guys like Wensink and Jonathan, and then [Al] Secord. If anything happened in Boston, who was going to take care of it on the Flyers? Me. There was too many of you guys.

DON: You said that the night before you played Boston, you couldn't sleep.

DAVE: Again, it was the anticipation that something was going to happen. It was different if a team had one guy. Most teams had one guy, maybe two, but you guys had three or four. The fans in Boston were tough to play in front of, and you hear their coach is nuts.

DON: That's true.

DAVE: I just didn't want to think about it. I would check the schedule sometimes two weeks in advance and saw Boston; I just didn't want to think about it because it would bother me for those two weeks.

DON: Now, you got 20 goals and you never played the power play. I really believe the Flyers got rid of you too soon. Did you resent that everybody in Philly called you the enforcer?

DAVE: Not at the time. I knew that if I didn't improve my skills, whether it was my defensive or offensive play, they certainly didn't rely on my goal-scoring skills, even though I did score here and there and I felt I could have scored more if given the chance. If I didn't improve as a hockey player, somebody would come along that was as tough and as big with more hockey skills, and he would replace me—and that's what happened when Paul Holmgren came along. But at the time, I was on such a roll with the success of the Flyers that coincided with our reputation, and I was just doing my thing. I didn't resent it at all.

DON: I have been in hockey a long time—I've never seen two guys [like you and Terry O'Reilly] go at it, not dirty, no sticks or anything. For about four years, you two guys went at it every time. I know Terry had a lot of respect for you.

DAVE: I had a lot of respect for Terry. I respect him beyond his aggressive style, but he went on to score a lot of goals and from what I heard, [he was] a real team leader. I certainly respected him, but it just seemed like any time something happened on the ice we got together.

When Dave and Terry were on the ice, no quarter was asked and no quarter was given.

TERRY O'REILLY

The Ultimate Bruin. Terry "Taz" O'Reilly after our
interview on the *Grapevine* show.

DAVE "THE HAMMER" SCHULTZ DID have it tough when
he played Boston. Over his career, Dave fought a Bruin at
least 14 times. He was right that there were a lot of guys
ready for Dave—or any of the Flyers, if they were looking for
trouble. We had Stan Jonathan, John Wensink, Al Secord
and Wayne Cashman, but mostly Terry "Taz" O'Reilly.

When many NHL fans think of personal rivalries, they
think of Bob Probert and Tie Domi. Bob and Tie had
three great fights that live on in hockey lore, but their
rivalry was not as fierce as the one between O'Reilly and
Schultz. When Philly visited the Garden, the Bruins fans
were abuzz, and when Terry and Dave were on the ice,

there was the air of anticipation you'd find at a heavy-weight title fight.

O'Reilly and Schultz seemed to be on the ice together a lot. In their careers, they went at it seven times, and that's just in the NHL. They had a few goes when they were in the American Hockey League.

Terry's nickname, Taz, was short for the Tasmanian Devil, the Warner Bros. cartoon character. The Tasmanian Devil would always be spinning, whirling, smashing and breaking things; he looked like Terry going into the corner after a puck.

Like Dave, the first time I saw Terry was in 1972, when I was coaching Rochester in the American League. Terry was 20 years old and was playing for the Bruins' farm team, the Boston Braves. The Bruins had drafted Terry in the first round, 14th overall, of the 1971 draft. I knew Terry was a pretty high pick, and when I saw him, I thought, "How could they draft this guy so high? He can't even skate."

We had Terry on the *Grapevine* show in 1985, six years after I left Boston. That year, the Bruins were beaten in the first round by Montreal, and Terry had missed a few games with a dislocated shoulder.

DON: Okay, Terry, tell everybody where you live.

TERRY: Well, the street I live on changed its name.

DON: Really? You're kidding.

TERRY: Yeah, it's 1 Cheevers Lane. [Gerry Cheevers was the Bruins coach that year.]

DON: Come on, tell everybody.

TERRY: It was 1 Cherry Street.

DON: How's your shoulder?

TERRY: It's coming along. I had it fixed after our short playoff stint. Once you dislocate your shoulder, it will keep coming out unless you have it surgically repaired.

DON: Well, when I was 20, I had my shoulder broken and I had it fixed, all wired up, and I came back and played the next 16 years with it—not very good though. Terry, I hope you play another 16 years.

TERRY: I hope so. Geez, Don, it must have been tough playing in those open-air rinks with a sore shoulder.

DON: Oh, is that so? Well, I saw you play in the American League and you were the worst skater in the world, no joke.

TERRY: Well, I have to say Terry Crisp was a worse skater.

DON: Funny, two redheaded guys. The next year, you were a pretty good skater. What the heck did you do over the summer to improve so much?

TERRY: I slept with my skates. I was not a good skater and my skating still could be better. The kids today there are getting so much good training at such an early age. When I played minor hockey, I played goalie until I was 12 years old. I never went to any hockey schools. I didn't know what my inside edge was or what my outside edge was, and the only way I stopped was smacking into the boards.

DON: There was usually someone in front of you when you smacked into the boards. Honestly, I thought when you played for the Braves that you were going to kill yourself.

TERRY: I skated a lot in the summers in the early part of my career. I knew that if I didn't do that, I wouldn't be playing professional hockey.

DON: In my first year, the Bruins had a Christmas party and everybody had to get a gag or joke gift. Tell us what the players gave you.

TERRY: I have about 12 pairs of double runner skates. They also gave me a pair of hockey pants with blades sewed on the seat of the pants.

Terry was not happy getting that gag gift at the Christmas party. I got a gag gift as well. That year, I talked a lot about John Wensink, who I coached in Rochester the year before, and how John was a tough player. I also talked a lot about my beloved bull terrier, Blue. So for my gag gift they gave me a little Yorkshire terrier puppy with a big collar around it engraved with the name John. I took the dog home, and Blue wasn't too happy. The next day, I brought the dog to the rink and one of the trainers took it home. In fact, just about every player was mad after they got their gift, so we stopped that gag gift stuff and just had a Christmas party at our favourite restaurant in Boston (actually it's in Saugus, Massachusetts), Kowloon, with no gifts.

I can honestly say I have never seen a player improve over his career as much as Terry O'Reilly. Terry went from a player so bad at skating you were afraid he was going to hurt himself falling into the boards, to leading a first-place NHL team in points six years later. Terry went from scoring 17 points in the AHL to scoring 90 in the NHL. There is a secret to Terry's success, and it can be summed up in two words: hard work.

> **DON:** I have to say, in our practice, you set the pace. Did you mean to do that, or was it just natural?

> **TERRY:** I felt that, going into a game, if I hadn't worked my brains out in practice two or three days before the game, I never had a real good feeling going into the game, so for me, working in practice before a game was very important. The thing that gave me and the team stamina—I don't know if you know it, but when you were coaching, remember what you called Black Tuesday? Well, I don't know if you called it that, but we sure did. We'd have a game on Thursday and then we'd play on the weekends, so Saturday and Sunday we played. Monday, Tuesday

and Wednesday were practice days, and then we'd start again, playing Thursday, Saturday and Sunday. Sometimes Monday would be an optional, depending on how we did on the weekend. Then Tuesday would be Black Tuesday. You'd skate us so hard when we got off the ice, we were almost physically sick. Over and backs and up and downs. When we go into the games on Thursday and the weekend games, everybody on the team knew, maybe it was a physiological thing, but we could go one level higher than the guy across from me because we worked harder during the week.

That is exactly why I skated them like that every Tuesday. One game in Buffalo, we beat them pretty good, and one of the players on the Sabres said, "If we worked as hard as the Bruins, we'd have won tonight." After a game in Atlanta, one of their reports said, "The Bruins played as if they were in a frenzy." We might lose, but we were not going to be outworked, and if you play that style of game, you'd better be in good shape.

The players would line up against the boards and do over and backs. Once, I did a Black Tuesday on the road. The arena we were practising in complained to Harry Sinden because we did so many over and backs that we shaved the ice down almost to the cement. Nobody cheated, and if you've ever done over and backs, you know what I mean — everybody touched the boards. One day, I drove them so hard that Don Marcotte was on his knees and said, "No more, Grapes." The one thing that the players knew was that I was not doing this to punish them, but to have them ready for the upcoming games.

I got the idea from my old coach in Rochester, Joe Crozier. We were practising at the Stamford Arena in Niagara Falls, Ontario, and Joe was mad at us for some reason. He made us do over and backs for what seemed like forever. Guys were on their knees, and I kept telling them to get up and not give Joe the satisfaction of seeing us quit. He was doing it to punish us, but in the back of my mind I knew it was what we needed at the time.

* * *

Terry would never talk about his fights. When a reporter asked about them, he said, "I'd rather talk about the goals."

On the ice, Terry wouldn't start a fight unless you bothered him or a teammate. If you did something to Terry's teammate, he took it personally. If anything happened on the ice, we never cried about it in the press or looked to the NHL to suspend the player. We felt like it was *our* job to punish the player that did something to one of our teammates, not the NHL's. I know that's a lot different than today.

A classic example was Thursday, March 9, 1978, in Detroit. We had beaten Detroit seven of the last eight games we played them. In our last game, we had 32 shots in the second period alone, so we pretty much had our way with Detroit.

One of our most reliable defencemen was Gary Doak. Gary was from Goderich, Ontario, and he was five foot ten and 185 pounds soaking wet. He had a bad habit when he went behind the net. Instead of just continuing around the net, he would stop behind the net, then turn back and try to go the other way. Today, they call it reversing the flow. I call it dumb. You are really asking to get creamed into the boards when you do that. I told Gary, "You keep doing that and someday you're going to get it." Well, this game was someday. Gary went behind the net, and instead of just going around the net, he turned back—or "reverses the flow," as Ron MacLean would say—and the Wings' Dennis Hextall was coming the other way. Hextall showed no mercy and just crushed Gary's head against the boards. Gary was knocked unconscious, got a 16-stitch cut and suffered a bad concussion and a broken orbital bone. No penalty.

I was furious. First, at Doaky. He was in the dressing room, blood running down his head, and I started to give him a hard time. "I told you not to do that, but you don't listen." I felt bad after. I shouldn't have given hell to a guy getting stitched for 16 good ones. When the press came in, I was still steaming. "The Big Bad Bruins—run them into the boards, hook 'em, rough 'em up, and you're just protecting your manhood. How come they don't play like that back in Boston?" I said it with as much sarcasm as I could. I went on to push the "us against the world" scenario: "Too bad about Doak. He's in the hospital . . . if it had been one of us, we would have had the penalty. But that's what happens when you are the Bruins."

That was true. If it were Terry who had hit someone like that, he would have gotten at least a game. Today, that hit would have cost Hextall 10 games or more, and he didn't even get two minutes for boarding. We didn't whine to the NHL about the hit or that there was no penalty. We'd handle it.

We didn't play the Wings until the next season. It was in Detroit and I had to fill out my lineup first. I had the line of Peter McNab, Donny Marcotte and Terry. For whatever reason, Wings coach Bobby Kromm, after he saw my starting lineup, started Hextall. Maybe he was trying to make a statement that they weren't scared. I never had to say anything about what happened the year before or what happened to Doak. The puck dropped, and 40 seconds in, Terry grabbed Hextall and gave it to him good. The next season, Dennis went to Washington, and the first time we played them, Stan Jonathan gave it to Hextall. Sending the message to the whole league.

In this book, Larry Zeidel called me polite because, just before I got into a fight, I'd ask a guy if he wanted to go. Terry was even more polite. Terry always fought fair and square. For instance, he would always tap a guy on the shoulders, and then the guy would turn around so that they could fight face to face. I told him, "Terry, one day you're going to tap a guy on the shoulder and some guy is going to turn around and sucker you."

> **DON:** Remember how you use to tap guys on the shoulder? This used to bug me when I first got to Boston. You'd tap the guy on the shoulder, the guy would turn around and they would be face to face. Then you dropped the gloves, you win the fight and we'd get the extra two minutes. I told you someday you'll

be sorry for doing that. Do you remember what happened in LA?

TERRY: Dan Maloney—boy, did he clock me. I had hit Butch Goring, who's not a big guy, but I hit him clean as the whistle went. Butch was cutting across the blue line and it was offside and I smacked into him on the whistle. I thought nothing of it, you know, I didn't feel bad about the play. I saw Dan Maloney skating towards me and talking to me. What he was saying was, "If you touch him, I'm going to kill you." I didn't know what he was saying, so I leaned forward to hear him better, and bang, he rocked me. I couldn't see after the first one hit me in the nose, tears rolling down and all.

The next time they played, Terry and Dan went at it again and this time Terry wasn't polite and got Dan back.

I never said a word when Terry came to the bench, which infuriated him even more. One story goes that he was in a fight with Dave "Tiger" Williams and when they fell to the ice, Terry said to Dave, "Put your head under my arm." Dave said, "What?" Terry said, "Just do it, because Cashman is coming and he's going to kick you in the head."

* * *

In my coaching career, there are a few goals that I can remember like they were scored yesterday, and Terry got one of those goals on double overtime against the Flyers in the 1977 Stanley Cup semifinals.

> **DON:** Okay, you better get this right. What was the most memorable goal you ever scored?

> **TERRY:** We were playing Philadelphia and we were in the second overtime. We had beat them the night before in an overtime, if I'm not mistaken.

> **DON:** Yes, Ricky Middleton scored.

> **TERRY:** It was a few years after they had beat us out of the playoffs, so we had a good rivalry going. You made a mistake and put me out in overtime.

> **DON:** True story.

> **TERRY:** All the other right wingers were either tired or in the penalty box, so you said, "Terry, get out there."

> **DON:** What happened is Bobby Schmautz came off and you jumped on and you got the winner. Bobby Clarke should have had you, but [he] went with Ratelle and [you] shoved it home. I always say you only have so much happiness, and that was one of the happiest times in Boston.

> **TERRY:** I remember Bobby Clarke breaking his stick over the crossbar.

There were four goals I remember most from my time coaching Boston. One was Terry's goal against the Flyers, and the others were Stan Jonathan and Gregg Sheppard's goals against the LA Kings, and of course Bobby Schmautz in Game 4 of the 1978 Stanley Cup finals.

Before we played Philly in the 1977 semifinals, we played LA in the quarter-finals. Not only was the LA series a rough one, with Stan Jonathan and Dave Schultz getting into a beauty, but it was the highest-scoring series I had ever been involved in. In six games we scored 30 goals, led by Bobby Schmautz, who scored eight goals in six games and ended up leading the all scorers in the playoffs in goals with 11 goals. He also set a record by scoring his first seven goals on only eight shots on net. LA scored 24 goals that series, so you can imagine there were some pretty wild games.

The first two games were in the Garden, and we won 8–3 and 6–2 before we headed to LA for Game 3 at the Forum. At that time, the Forum was one of the loudest buildings in the NHL, and the LA fans were going crazy before the game. The Kings came out smoking and it was 3–1 after the first period. We came out hard in the second, and less than four minutes into the period we had tied up the game with goals by Terry and Donny Marcotte. LA came right back, and by the time the period ended, the Kings had scored two more and it was 5–3 going into the third.

Ten seconds into the third, Bobby Schmautz scored. Wayne Cashman scored about 10 minutes later to tie the game, and with less than three minutes left in the period

Don Marcotte scored his second goal of the game and we were up by one. The Forum fans were going nuts, and then less than a minute after Marcotte scored, LA's superstar, Marcel Dionne, tied the game at six. My heart sank— we'd worked so hard, battling back from 3–1 and 5–3 deficits. I've often said I never told the Bruins what to do in the offensive end of the ice except for one thing: shoot from anywhere. If a player had a shot and passed instead, it would drive me nuts. So Stan Jonathan did what I told all the players. He went down the wing, didn't have a great angle and let go a wicked wrist shot. It hit LA's great little goalie, Rogie Vachon. Rogie pulled off the post a bit and it hit his shoulder and bounced up under the crossbar and in, with 13 seconds left in the third period. I just about fainted.

So we had a 3–0 lead in games, the fourth game was in LA, and they were desperate—to me, it was a given that they were going to win. They won 7–4 and we headed back to Boston.

Vachon was getting roasted in the papers because he was letting in an average of six goals per game in the first four games. I ran into this before in the playoffs—a good goalie gets it in the press for playing bad and then comes back and stones us. Tony Esposito comes to mind. But I figured we'd wrap it up at home. Lo and behold, Rogie stoned us. We poured 40 shots on him and he let in one goal. Dave Schultz got the first goal for LA and we tied it up on a great goal from Rick Middleton. Still tied going into the third, when they got a lucky goal. Don Murdoch put an easy shot on net, our goalie, Gerry Cheevers, kicked the rebound out and it hit Brad Park's skate and rolled back into the net. What was even more maddening was that the winning goal was offside. Rogie did the rest and we were heading back 3,000 miles to LA.

Game 6, and if LA won and forced a Game 7 back in Boston, who knows what might've happened. The crowd in LA was going crazy, but we were all over the Kings in the first, and after 20 minutes we were up 3–0 and rolling along. We were still up 3–0 going into the third, and LA had hardly any shots on net. The Kings popped one in less than a minute into the period, and they tied it up with two more quick goals. We went on the power play and the puck went into the corner in the LA end. Dave Hutchison got the puck, and when he tried to blast it out of his end, his stick broke and the puck went to Gregg Sheppard, who moved in on Rogie Vachon. Bobby Schmautz, who had already scored seven goals in the series, was standing wide open by the side of the net. I thought Gregg was going to pass the puck to him, and so did Rogie, who pulled off the post. And then Gregg snapped it home, top corner. We held on and won the game 4–3. Like I said, if we had lost that game and headed back to Boston for Game 7, who knows?

Terry's goal in double overtime against Philly was just as memorable as the two goals against the Kings. Philly had knocked us out of the playoffs the year before in the semi-finals, so we were looking for some payback.

Before we get to Terry's goal, there was a strange thing that happened in the first game of that series.

We had played seven games in 14 days with over 12,000 miles of travel, while Philly had finished off the Toronto

Maple Leafs and they were fairly well rested. In the first game in Philly, we were up 3–0 after the first, but Bobby Clarke scored the game-tying goal with 29 seconds left in the third. Fred Shero had pulled the Flyers' goalie, Wayne Stephenson, in the third period and put in Bernie Parent, who had not played since the first two games against the Leafs in the quarter-finals. We didn't get many shots in the third, and I knew going into overtime that Parent was cold. I told the players to go out and give it all we had early, and if that was not enough, well, we tried. Again, I told the players to shoot from anywhere, to get some shots on Parent.

That's exactly what Rick Middleton did. Less than three minutes into the game, Rick went wide, past their defence, and blasted it on Parent. He fought the puck but made the save, and the puck got behind him. He fell down and reached back to clear the puck from the crease, and he accidentally knocked it into the net. Boy, there is nothing like stealing the first game of a playoff series on the road. Now all the pressure was on the Flyers for Game 2.

Game 2 in Philly was one of the more memorable games I coached. I knew Philly was desperate not to go down 2–0 because they played Kate Smith's "God Bless America"—the Flyers had a record of 49 wins and only five losses when they played Kate before a game. This game was so memorable because of how fast the goals came. We went up 1–0 on a goal by Peter McNab, and 68 seconds later André "The Moose" Dupont scored to tie the game. It was 3–1 Philly about halfway through the game. Gregg Sheppard scored to make it 3–2, and Mike Milbury scored a minute later to make it 3–3. Fifteen seconds after that, Gary Dornhoefer scored to put Flyers up 4–3. It was only another 23 seconds before Jean Ratelle scored to tie it at four. That set a record—three goals in 38 seconds—and we just missed setting another record when we scored four goals in 98 seconds.

The game went into double overtime for one reason: our goalie, Gerry Cheevers. One of the headlines in the paper read, AN IRISHMAN [Terry] SHALL LEAD THEM BUT A SCOTSMAN [Cheevers] WILL KEEP THEM IN THE GAME. Gerry was unbelievable, facing over 50 shots. It's funny how goalies seem to have teams' numbers. Gerry seemed to have Philly's number; he always played well against the Flyers.

In the *Grapevine* interview with Terry, he joked that all the other right wingers were tired or in the penalty box, and that was pretty much true. I was asked after the game about putting Terry on the ice for the goal, and I said, "Terry was taking an extra half shift when he scored. Schmautz looked tired but Taz was hyper and he wanted to go so I put him out there with Ratelle and Marcotte." Terry jumped on the ice and headed straight for the net, and the puck went into the corner. Bobby Clarke went to cover Ratelle, and that left Terry wide open in front of their net. Don Marcotte got the puck in the corner, put it out to Terry, and he slipped it past Wayne Stephenson. I remember Bobby Clarke taking his stick and smashing it over the crossbar too. There was a great picture of Terry with his hand raised in victory as Clarke is smashing his stick. I have the picture in my den and still look at it every day.

When we returned home from Philly, the players' wives and Rose met us at the airport. Peter McNab's wife,

Diana, came over and said, "That's great, Don, winning both games."

I said, "Yep, Diana, outcoached them again."

She hit me with her purse.

*   *   *

I have often said that all I wanted my wingers to do was to cover the points in our end of the ice. That way, as soon as our defencemen got the puck they could, without even thinking, put it around the boards or off the glass and a winger would be there to make sure it got out of our end of the ice. Every winger covered the points at all costs, except Terry. Peter McNab, Terry's centreman and good friend, said, "I feel sorry for the opposition; they have no idea where Terry's going because *we* have no idea where Terry's going."

He was murder on the defence. He'd just come out of nowhere. The one problem we had is we didn't know what Terry was going to do in our end of the ice. So, what was the secret to my success with Terry? I just let him go.

I'd try to get Terry to cover the points, but to no avail. In practice, I would call over Terry and defencemen like Rick Smith and I'd say, "Okay, Rick, you got the puck in the corner. Do you want Terry out at the point or do you want him in the corner shaking hands with you?" All the defencemen would say, "At the point."

When Terry wouldn't cover the points and we got scored on and the play started with the defenceman that Terry should have been covering, I would be steaming behind the bench. But I had to be very careful about how I handled Terry. I paced up and down the bench, saying, "Yes, everybody else covers the point, but not Terry. No, no, Terry knows better." The players on the bench would just put their heads down—they dared not laugh. Later, Terry told me that when I was doing that, he had to grab the cuff of his hockey pants because he was so mad that he didn't want to jump and choke me. I knew that you didn't go one on one with Terry and embarrass him.

I was often criticized for not stopping Terry from fighting and getting a lot of penalties. He was our leading scorer one year, and I was often asked by the reporters, "Wouldn't it be better if Terry didn't fight? Then he would be on the ice more."

"You can't take the teeth out of a tiger and still expect him to be a tiger" was always my response.

Off the ice, like most tough guys, he was very quiet and had an unusual hobby.

> **DON:** So, tell us what you do when you are away from the rink.

> **TERRY:** Well, not much. I guess you mean the stained glass. Well, I like to make stained-glass windows. I think it's because I like to break a lot of glass.

Last season, I went to a celebration of the 40th anniversary of the Bruins having eleven 20-goal scorers, an NHL record never broken. The Bruins and Rick Middleton did a great job organizing the event. Before the Calgary–Boston game, they introduced each player, and the biggest cheer was for Terry O'Reilly. South Boston is mostly Irish, and they loved the Bruins, and especially Terry O'Reilly. He was the ultimate Bruin: he was tough, he hit and fought, he scored goals and stood up for his teammates.

I remember seeing Terry O'Reilly and Dave Schultz at a banquet years ago. Both were the same: very quiet gentlemen. It was only when they hit the ice that you'd yell, "Look out!"

BOB KELLY

Bob "Battleship" Kelly—one of the
toughest players ever to play the game.

IN A LATER CHAPTER, I TALK about how I wanted my teams
to play like Blue: full out, in a frenzy and with attitude. But
let me tell you, that's a tough way to play. It makes it easier
when you have the toughest guy in the league on your
bench. Teams look at you differently when you have the
heavyweight champ on your team.

In 1972 I was made the coach and general manager of
the Rochester Americans. We were an independent team
with no NHL affiliate, which meant we didn't have any
players for months before the season started. I knew the
kind of team I wanted to create. I wasn't going to get a lot
of goal scoring, so I figured I would try and get one or

maybe two goal scorers and then load up on tough guys. Not just fighters, but guys who would work hard and bang and crash. And I wanted a heavyweight, so I set my sights on Bob "Battleship" Kelly.

In September of that year, I went to all the different NHL training camps to see if I could pick up guys that were on their way to leagues below the American Hockey League. One camp I went to was the New York Rangers' camp in Peterborough, Ontario. I got there nice and early, and as I walked up to the door I saw a sign that said, PLAYERS AND MANAGEMENT ONLY. I started to limp and the guard said, "Tough practice yesterday?"

I nodded.

No one was on the ice except the Rangers' coach, Emile Francis, who was working with the goalies. He gave me a slight nod and I sat in the stands and watched the practices that day. A friend of mine, Dennis Ball, was the assistant GM of the Rangers at the time. I told him I was looking for some players and asked if he had any that might be available. Dennis said he'd talk to Emile and see what he could do. The next day, Dennis and Emile came through big and gave me some very good players. Emile Francis told Dennis he was impressed that I would be at the rink so early, and so he wanted to help me. I owe Dennis and Emile a big thank you.

The Rangers owned Battleship's rights, and I asked if he was available. Dennis said, "Do you really want Battleship? I heard that he tried to punch out his coach a few years ago." Sounds just like the guy I wanted! Dennis told me that Battleship was promised to Baltimore of the AHL. I tried to talk Dennis into changing his mind, but Battleship was off the table.

I was happy with the team I built. We had a good goalie in Lynn Zimmerman, a few guys who could score like Barry Merrell, Larry McKillop and Herman Karp. But at the start of the season we would have 10 guys who never played a professional game. We had some tough guys like Rod Graham, John Bednarski and Bob Malcolm, but we didn't have a heavyweight forward. To me, that was still the missing piece of the puzzle.

I can still remember the call. I was sitting at home in the living room and the phone rang. It was Dennis. He told me the team Battleship was going to refused to pay his $500 signing bonus. If I wanted Battleship I would have to give him the 500 bucks and money for a bus ticket to Rochester. I said, "Dennis, he's got the five hundred, and if he wants, I'll go down and carry Battleship to Rochester on my back." I was so excited I actually jumped up and down after hanging up the phone.

Bob "Battleship" Kelly was six foot two and 190 pounds, and he came from Fort William (now Thunder Bay), Ontario. He was drafted in the second round of the 1967 NHL Amateur Draft by the Leafs. Bob spent the next five years with six different teams in the American, International and Central League. He was 26 years old and was mostly used as a mad dog by the other coaches. He had developed a fearsome reputation as one of the toughest fighters in the minor leagues.

I could relate to what Bob was going through. I'd also spent years in the minors, and your dream of making the

NHL starts to fade. It's even tougher when you sit at the end of the bench and then you're sent on the ice to fight. When Battleship came to training camp, I told him I was going to play him on a regular shift and he was going to play the power play. I explained to him he wouldn't have to fight all the time—just being on the ice and staring at guys and pushing them after the whistle was enough most times. I said to Bob, "Listen to me, you could be the heavy-weight champ of the American League, and if you score goals, the NHL would have to take a look and you'll make it to the NHL."

You have to remember, this was back in 1972. The Rochester War Memorial didn't have glass around the boards; it still had a wire fence. The benches were on opposite sides of the ice and there was only one penalty box. There was no music between plays, and we didn't even have an organist or a mascot. The fans were there just to watch hockey, without all the bells and whistles of today's game. The Rochester fans and press, especially Hans Tanner of the *Democrat and Chronicle*, were great with us that season.

We played well at the start of the season, even putting together some winning streaks, and the fans started to pack the building. Bob got off to a good start as well, scoring a few goals. He didn't even fight for the first six or seven games because no one wanted to fight him. The AHL was tough back then because you had players fighting to get to the NHL and guys who had been in the NHL and been sent down, and they were fighting to get back up. It was only a matter of time before Battleship showed up. It happened at home, in a game against the Cincinnati Swords.

It was the middle of the third period and Bob Kelly and the Swords' Jake Rathwell were skating for the puck at centre ice. Rathwell brought his stick up and hit Kelly in the mouth and gave him a beauty cut. Kelly went to his knees and the play went on down the ice. When the play came back up the ice, Kelly grabbed Rathwell and really gave it to him. The fans went nuts. Both were sent to the penalty box. A guy named Bob Wetmore was the penalty box attendant, and he sat between Kelly and Rathwell. One thing led to another and they went at it again, and Kelly really gave Jake a beating. Wetmore was quoted in an article in a Rochester paper as saying he had a brand new London Fog raincoat that was ruined by the blood splattered all over it. With the fight in the penalty box, the fans went nuts again and the legend of Battleship Kelly was born, along with a love affair with the Rochester fans.

* * *

Battleship was one of the most feared guys in the league, and that made our whole team grow about an inch. His fearsome reputation grew when we were on the road and, during the warm-up, we ran out of pucks—shot 'em all over the glass, or I guess I should say the fence. In those days, you stayed on your side of the centre line and didn't dare cross over to the other half of the ice. Bob skated down into the other team's end, pushed the goalie out of the way and shot a bunch of pucks down to our end. Nobody said a word.

In the War Memorial, the big American flag hung at our end of the ice, and when the national anthem was played the visiting team would be looking at the backs of the Rochester starting lineup. I would always start Battleship, and halfway through the anthem Bob would take off his right glove and start to run his hand through his hair. His hand would be taped up, and he was showing the other team that he was ready if any trouble started. After a while, the Amerk fans came to love the sight of him running his taped hand through his hair.

The two top gunslingers that year were Battleship and the New Haven Nighthawks' Kevin Morrison. It was only a matter of time before they met and settled once and for all who was the AHL heavyweight champ. We were in the same conference and ahead of New Haven by about 10 points. They had a tough team led by Kevin, Garry Howatt and Bob Nystrom. We had a few tough games with them, but this one was a beauty. It was February 28, 1973, and by the time the game ended we had eight minors, six fighting majors and two 10-minute misconducts, and New Haven had five minors, six fighting majors and two 10-minute misconducts.

In the first period, Kelly and Morrison started to push and shove, but for some reason, the linesmen jumped in and separated them. The fans started to boo and were egging Kelly and Morrison on. Other than that little bit of pushing and shoving, the game was tame until the third period. At the four-minute mark, Rochester's—and my—good buddy Rod Graham battled with the Hawks' Garry Howatt. During that fight, Kelly and Morrison stepped back from the crowd of players and dropped their gloves. It was like a scene out of the Old West between two gunslingers. You couldn't hear yourself think because of the New Haven fans' screaming and yelling; they had been waiting for this the whole game. Battleship and Morrison went toe to toe, throwing bombs. Kelly hit Kevin hard and often.

Kevin grabbed hold of Battleship and they fell to the ice with Battleship on top, throwing punches. Normally, the linesmen would jump in and break up the fight, but I think they were mad after getting an earful from the fans when they broke them up earlier in the game, so they decided to let them go. Kevin and Battleship got back to their skates, nodded at each other and went at it again. Battleship had his right hand free and landed some beauties, and they ended up along the boards with Bob raining down punches. The fight was one-sided. Kevin's fiancée came running down from the stands and started yelling at us, calling us a bunch of animals.

When Battleship came to the bench, I grabbed his hand and raised it, like they do to show who's the winner of a boxing match. I told him to go for a skate with his hands raised in victory. The fans went bananas. They were throwing things on the ice, and then they started to pull the armrests from the seats and throw them on the ice.

Rochester's fans loved our team and Battleship. The year before, there were 60,000 fans at the Amerks games. That year, with Battleship, we had over 200,000 in attendance, the first time in Rochester history the attendance topped 150,000. After the season, one of Rochester's owners, Bob Clarke, came into my office. He paced up and down and said to me, "Don, we have a problem with the attendance."

I couldn't believe what I was hearing. "Bob, we were jammed to the rafters this season. What do you mean you have a problem with the attendance?"

Bob started to laugh. "Well, we budgeted for a loss of $200,000 this season and we *made* over $200,000, and now we have a tax problem."

* * *

Besides being the AHL heavyweight champ, Bob went on to score 27 goals and 62 points. I knew the NHL would come knocking. Sure enough, St. Louis bought his contract from us. Finally, after six years in the minors, Battleship made it to the NHL.

When Bob left for St. Louis, he bought my daughter, Cindy, a small television as a thank-you gift.

Years later, Emile Francis, who owned Battleship's rights in New York, was asked about letting him go, since Bob went on to make an impact in the NHL. He said, "You can only have so many tough guys, and I think we had enough with the Rangers, particularly at that time. There's always a case that we could have misjudged him. I mean, it wouldn't have been the first mistake we ever made—that can happen in hockey. You know, sometimes someone has to go somewhere else to get that break and really come out and prove what he can do. Bob sure did under Don. I mean, I thought Don did a tremendous job with that team."

John Muckler, who went on to win five Stanley Cups with the Oilers, was coaching the Providence Reds when

Battleship was in Rochester. He said, "Kelly was the meanest and best enforcer at that time. He was fearless, and of course, big. He's strong. He knew how to fight. A lot of people really feared him. I'd have to rate him up there with [Dave] Semenko, who I coached in Edmonton."

Battleship made his presence known in the NHL in an exhibition game in St. Louis. The Blues were playing the Broad Street Bullies, and you know who Kelly was gunning for: the Hammer. Midway through the first period, Kelly and Dave Schultz went at it, and Battleship, by all accounts, won the fight. After their penalties were up, they stepped out of the box and immediately dropped the gloves, and again, most gave the nod to Kelly. It quickly went around the league that you should not mess with Battleship. When Schultz was asked once to name the best fighters he had fought, he mentioned Terry O'Reilly and Battleship, along with Clark Gillies, Behn Wilson and Garry Howatt.

Halfway through Bob's first year in St. Louis, he was traded to Pittsburgh, where he became a huge fan favourite. When he went on the ice, the organist would play "Anchors Aweigh." The local Navy Recruiting Command gave Battleship an honorary membership. In his three full seasons with the Penguins, Bob scored 62 goals, 137 points and over 380 minutes in penalties, as well as eight points in nine games in the Penguins' 1975 playoff run.

* * *

On January 23, 1974, Rose, Cindy, Tim and I went up to St. Louis to see the Blues play the Penguins. The Blues had called up John Wensink, who I had in Rochester that season. I needed an enforcer to replace Battleship and I got John, who fit the bill. The Blues owned John's contract, and they called him up to help get some toughness into the lineup against the Penguins—this was just after they traded for Battleship. John was only 20 years old and was not ready to tangle with a guy like Battleship. I was hoping that if they did go, Kelly would let up on John. I got Rose, Cindy and Tim tickets in the first row, along the glass, in the corner, while I sat somewhere else.

John and Bob didn't get into it, but early in the second period, Battleship and Barclay Plager of the Blues dropped the gloves. As the linesmen were breaking up that fight, the Blues' Bob Gassoff and Pittsburgh's Steve Durbano got into it right in front of Rose, Tim and Cindy. Gassoff was a good-looking guy with long, curly blond hair. He looked like Brad Pitt in that movie *Troy*. Steve Durbano was a tough-looking guy, and his nickname was "Mental Case" Durbano. Both guys were as tough as they come. Durbano cut Gassoff, and there was blood all over his blond hair. Then Durbano grabbed Gassoff's hair and smashed his head against the glass. Gassoff grabbed Durbano and head-butted him. After all was said and done, there was some blood on the glass and blood on the ice.

After the game, we were all going out for dinner. When I asked Rose where she wanted to go, she said, "I don't want to go out for dinner. I have a headache."

Now, that's not like Rose, but then I put two and two together. "Oh, I get it; you're upset about that fight right in front of you."

Rose said, "Yes. What that Durbano did to that good-looking young man, it was awful."

Now, Rose had seen me in a lot of fights and the aftermath of the fights, but never up close. She always saw it from far away in the stands, and that was the first time she'd been up close and experienced the violence of a fight, and that was a violent fight. So we didn't have any dinner that night.

* * *

Bob "Battleship" Kelly went on to play over 400 games in the NHL, earning almost 200 career points. He was one of the toughest guys ever to play the game, and when I got him in Rochester, I knew we were going to be successful. And that success got me a shot at coaching the Bruins.

JOHN FERGUSON

The Montreal Canadiens' John Ferguson was the ultimate enforcer.

FROM JUNIOR HOCKEY TO THE NHL

WHEN WE HEAR ABOUT TOUGH GUYS in the NHL, we think of players like Ryan Reaves, Tom Wilson, Bob Probert, Tie Domi, and further back Dave Schultz and Terry O'Reilly, but one of the toughest guys ever to play in the NHL was John Ferguson of the Montreal Canadiens. John was born in 1938 in Vancouver, British Columbia, and was raised by his mother after his father died when John was just nine years old. John began earning his reputation as a tough guy in junior, but he was a tough guy that could still put pucks in the net.

John played junior hockey in the Saskatchewan Junior League for the Melville Millionaires, where he led the team with 66 points and 83 penalty minutes in just 44 games. The road to the NHL was different for players back in John's day. Today, you see 18-year-old kids come right from junior hockey and make the NHL. That was not so when John was a junior. You had to pay your dues.

DON: Okay, John, I'm going to start you off with a tough question: Where were you born and raised?

JOHN: Vancouver, B.C.

DON: You were a Fort William boy, weren't you? How did you get hooked up with Connie Madigan?

JOHN: No, we played together in Fort Wayne. There is a genuine tough guy.

DON: You better believe it—Mad Dog Connie Madigan. My defence partner, and believe me, he was tough.

JOHN: Talking about tough hockey clubs, my first club out of junior hockey, I go to the Vancouver Canucks' training camp [in the old Western Hockey League]. First day of training camp, Art Chapman came into the dressing room and said, "I'm sending you to Fort Wayne, where you were last year." I told him I was in junior hockey last year.

DON: He didn't even know where you played last year. That must have given you confidence.

JOHN: It's the last day of training camp and it's going well. So I had a good reputation in junior, and I'm playing pretty well in the big team — Vancouver's — camp and I'm thinking I made it. We are flying in a small 16-seater plane, I guess we carried a small roster, and we were going to Victoria to play the Cougars in the first game of the season. At that time, Danny Belisle, who was a pretty good goal scorer, was holding out for a contract. The coach came to me and tapped me on the shoulder and said, "Danny just signed and you're going to Fort Wayne." I went to Fort Wayne, and my first room-mate was Connie Madigan.

DON: That was a treat.

JOHN: Yeah, really, that was a treat. We had the toughest minor-league club ever.

DON: Who was on it?

JOHN: Well, we had Paul Strasser, Andy Voykin and Art Hart. Art was the light-heavyweight champion of Canada when he played on that team. Another tough guy was Eddie Long — boy, we had some scrappers.

DON: I played on one of the toughest teams in the minors when I was in Spokane, playing for the Comets. We had Connie "Mad Dog" Madigan, Bill "The

Destroyer" Shvetz, Sandy "Stone Face" Hucul. I was like a baby on that team. But you almost ended up going to college instead of playing junior hockey. What happened?

JOHN: I played junior in Melville, Saskatchewan, and I had a scholarship to go to Colorado College or the University of North Dakota. I had signed a C form.

DON: Tell the people about the C form.

JOHN: For $100, you signed a C form and the pro team owned your rights. You couldn't go to school because you had taken money from a professional team. Red Hay at that time was in North Dakota and wanted me. So that was the story. I couldn't go to school, and I went on to Fort Wayne.

DON: You made it to Montreal. Tell us about your linemates the first game. Not too shabby.

JOHN: My first game was in the Boston Garden, and my linemates were "Boom Boom" Geoffrion and Jean Béliveau.

DON: How did you do? Did you score?

JOHN: I got two.

DON: Two. I bet they thought "The Rocket" has returned.

JOHN: It was a great thrill, and after one game I was leading the National Hockey League in goals.

The next day, the headlines in the paper were OPENING NIGHT PRODUCES NEW STAR. Not only did John get two goals, but he assisted on a goal by Geoffrion in a 4–4 tie in Boston. So three points in a 4–4 tie, in his first game, not bad.

The first time I saw John Ferguson was when he was playing for the Cleveland Barons of the American Hockey League. Boy, was he tough. He would run on his skates and when he got near you, he'd jump. If you tried to hit him, you'd pay the price. He took no prisoners. Sam Pollock, the genius behind the Montreal Canadiens, saw that he needed an enforcer for Jean Béliveau. Jean was the star of the team, making the big money, and teams were taking shots at him. Sam was the first guy to bring up an enforcer, and that was John Ferguson. Everybody knew John was tough and what he was there for, and so to make a point, the Canadiens started him on the wing with Jean. Yes, John scored, but what he didn't tell us was that, 12 seconds into his first NHL game, he dropped the gloves with Ted Green and got into not one, but two fights that night. So John really had two goals, an assist and two fights. Not a bad debut.

John certainly made an impression on Jean Béliveau. Jean was quoted as saying, "For us, Fergy's greatest contribution was his spirit. He was the consummate team man and probably intimidated as many of us in the dressing room as he did opponents on the ice. You wouldn't dare give less than your best if you wore the same sweater as John Ferguson."

* * *

The three great old buildings in the Original Six era were Maple Leaf Gardens, Boston Garden and the Montreal Forum. Part of the mystique of the Forum was the Canadiens dressing room. In 1952, coach Dick Irvin had a verse from John McCrae's poem "In Flanders Fields" painted on the wall: *To you from failing hands we throw the torch; be yours to hold it high.*

When you played for the Montreal Canadiens, they treated you different than other teams.

> **DON:** I am always interested in what it's like for first-time Montreal players when they walk into the Forum and into the Canadiens dressing room.

> **JOHN:** Well, it's quite a thing for a young boy from out west. I had only been to the Forum once, to see an All-Star Game when I was playing in the American League for Cleveland. Walk into the dressing room and you see all the plaques with the picture of the Stanley Cup and the names of all the winners. There's quite a bit of history when you walk in there, and it's just a charming building. Of course, the big CH is there, and the "Flanders Field" quote. It really is something to see and be a part of.

> **DON:** I was at the Toronto camp, and they had the minor leaguers in one room, the rookies in another room, and we were like the dregs of society. Some of the

minor leaguers were next to the boiler room, and the room was always soaking wet. Now, in Montreal, I was there for a cup of coffee for the two weeks of their training camp, but I sat next to Jean Béliveau and another big star. They treat everybody great and treat everybody the same for the first two weeks.

JOHN: They certainly did back then. Right off the bat at training camp, they split everybody up into four teams and then they blow the whistle and drop the puck and you start to scrimmage the first day of training camp.

PLAYING FOR TOE BLAKE AND GOING UP AGAINST HULL

WHILE IN MONTREAL, JOHN PLAYED FOR maybe the greatest coach of all time, Hector "Toe" Blake. Toe was born in Victoria Mines, Ontario, which is now considered a ghost town, and in 1934 he made the Montreal Maroons. A year later he got traded to the Canadiens and played 13 seasons with them. He won three Stanley Cups, a Hart Trophy, a Lady Byng, was named to the First All-Star Team three times, led the league in scoring in 1938–39 and was voted as one of the greatest 100 players in NHL history. With all that, he's still best known for coaching the Montreal Canadiens while wearing his signature black fedora. In the 1955–56 season, five years after retiring, Toe coached the Montreal Canadiens to a Stanley Cup championship, the first of five in a row. Toe

Bobby Hull had one of the first curved sticks in hockey.
The curve on his stick got so crazy the NHL had to make a rule to reduce the size.

Fred Shero and Bobby Clarke in action.

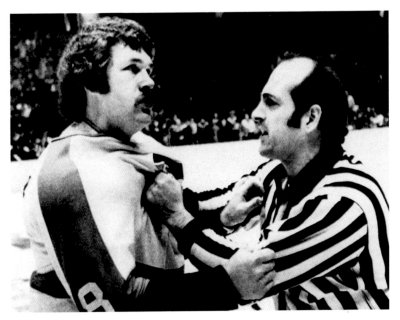

Dave "The Hammer" Schultz being held back by linesman John D'Amico.

I met Dave Schultz at the old Philadelphia Spectrum just days before it was torn down. Lots of memories in that old building, including Terry O'Reilly's double OT goal vs. the Flyers, and Philly vs. the Red Army.

Terry "Taz" O'Reilly's best year with me was in the '77–78 season, when he scored 90 points, 211 penalty minutes, 13 majors and was a +40.

John Ferguson was one of the toughest guys in hockey.
Here he is about to land a big right on the Rangers' Bob Nevin.

John Ferguson was the Team Canada GM and I was
the coach in the 1981 World Championship in Sweden.

TO DON:
WITH APPLAUSE AND APPRECIATION.
thanks for the
memories,
Szep

The Boston Globe

" CHEER UP, BLUE, YOUR OLD MAN DID SUPER "

A cartoon by Paul Szep that ran in The Boston Globe *after we lost Game 7 to Montreal in 1979. Everybody knew that Blue and I wouldn't be back in Boston the next year and Paul was saying goodbye. The autograph says: "To Don: With applause and appreciation. Thanks for the memories, Paul Szep."*

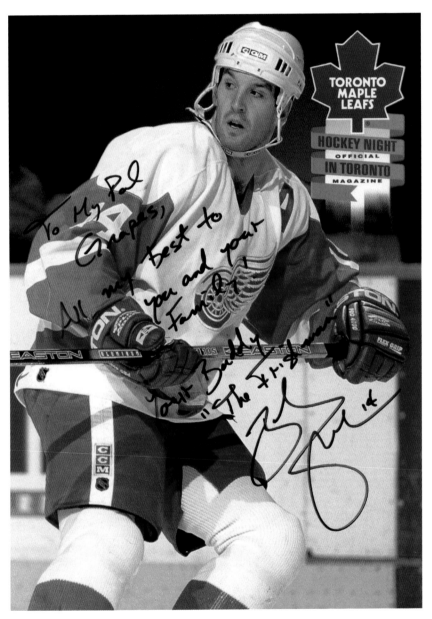

A tip of the hat to "a fine broth of a lad"
Brendan Shanahan for a great job with the Leafs.

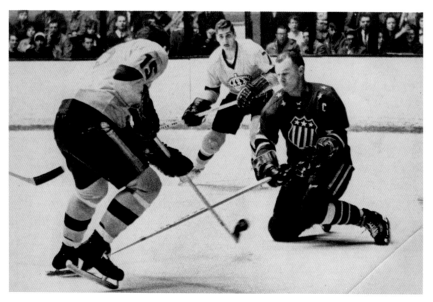

Me in action. We never thought it was going to end when we were playing.

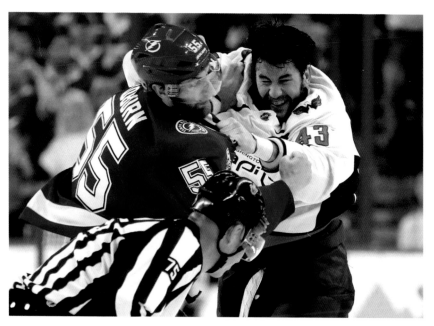

Capital Tom Wilson and Lightning Braydon Coburn go at it in Game 7 of the 2018 semifinals. Wilson was sticking up for Evgeny Kuznetsov after Coburn pulled his sweater off. You have to have guys on the team ready to stick up for the sweethearts.

This was taken at the 40th anniversary of the '77–78 Bruins who had eleven 20 or more goal scorers. From left to right: Rick Middleton, Gregg Sheppard, Terry O'Reilly (looks like Terry is about to hit me), me, Peter McNab and Bobby Miller.

Ron and me before the first game of the Stanley Cup finals.
That's George Salami's jacket I'm wearing.

ended up winning a total of eight Stanley Cups as the head coach of Montreal.

DON: Tell me what it was like playing for the great Toe Blake.

JOHN: He had a memory like an elephant. If you ever lost an important faceoff, you'd never take another one. He never made a mistake coaching; he was always ahead of the play and thinking. He was a player's coach in that he let you have a beer after a game. We travelled by the trains at the time, and we were in the smoker or private cars and he'd let you have a beer or two. He treated you like a man. The morning before every game, we'd have a pre-game meeting. In those days, if you went on the ice the morning of a game, it was just to get a feel for the ice or test your skates or something like that, but every game day we'd have a meeting. He was the boss—you never talk back to Toe. He was a great mastermind of the game.

DON: I go to practices nowadays and I see some of the practices, and you have to be Einstein to figure out what was going on. Now, Toe was the master—eight Stanley Cups in 13 years. What was one of Toe's practices like?

JOHN: Frankly, we started by skating backward. You'd start by skating backward for a half hour or so.

DON: No kidding?

JOHN: We did a lot of real game-like drills, line rushes, and we scrimmaged a lot. But the day before a game, we'd never scrimmage. Those practices were very tactical practices. He'd put the emphasis on, say, Mikita if we were playing Chicago or Ratelle's line if we were playing the Rangers. We'd really key in on the big lines before we played them.

DON: Back then, and even now, there is a lot of pressure for the team to win in Montreal.

JOHN: You definitely had to win in Montreal. When I played, there were five daily newspapers, two English and three French. You were always being interviewed and the papers were always playing one against the other. Controversy every week.

DON: The reporters were a little afraid of Toe . . .

JOHN: Oh, definitely. I think they were glad to see him go.

* * *

Now, John was an enforcer—that's for sure. If anybody touched Jean Béliveau, he'd better be prepared to suffer John's wrath. Fergy was going to make you pay. John was also a checker; he would check some of the other team's stars, especially the Chicago Blackhawks' Bobby Hull. John also had a few classic tilts with the Leafs' Eddie Shack. John could really throw them. When he got the right hand free, look out.

DON: Okay, you and Bobby Hull. Now, I was playing in Siberia somewhere and I heard about this fight with you and Bobby Hull. He had a broken jaw, he was bugging you and you were bugging him, so what happened?

JOHN: Well, we always played against Hull's line. Now, my linemate Claude Provost would check him and I always told him, "If Hull gets away from you, I'll crack him." One night in Chicago, he was coming across centre and I caught him with a shoulder.

DON: Stick down?

JOHN: Stick down. It was clean and I caught him pretty good. He got a broken jaw, amazingly enough. About two or three games later, he came into the Forum with a broken jaw and the lights were sparkling off his wired teeth and everything. A little scrum started, and he came right into the middle and one thing led to another. He ended up underneath me and I cocked my fist and was about to drill him and I thought to myself, "Fergy, if you hit him, you're the dirtiest rat in Canada."

DON: So, did you hit him?

JOHN: No, I didn't hit him. That scrum was played up in the papers the next day and it's still a big controversy today, and nothing really happened.

A MOVE TO COACHING AND THE 1980 NHL DRAFT

JOHN WASN'T LIKE ME. He was preparing for retirement and life after hockey. In the 1970–71 season, he had a pretty good year. He scored 30 points, had over 160 penalty minutes and won the Stanley Cup; at the end of the season, John just up and retired.

DON: Now, you're rolling along and everything is good, everybody figures you're going to go another five years, and all of the sudden, right out of the blue, you retired. What happened?

JOHN: Well, I had a business in Montreal and I had a couple of partners, and I guess I was making as much out[side] of the game as I was playing.

DON: So, what were you making back then?

JOHN: The last year I played, I was making $57,000, so it was good money.

DON: I was making 45 at the same time. Forty-five hundred. So, why did you retire?

JOHN: I had another year to go on my contract. But a lot of people were asking me to retire and my business started to grow. When everybody around is saying retire, you start to think, "Maybe I should." I was in the garment business and we went from 60 employees to a thousand, so I thought it was time.

* * *

John was involved with the '72 Summit Series as coach Harry Sinden's second in command. John was just as intense off the ice as he was on the ice. Team Canada was having a hard time at the start of the series, and after they had lost a game, Harry and John got on an elevator at their hotel. Some guy got on the elevator with them and started to give Harry a hard time about losing the game. John reached over Harry, grabbed the guy by the tie, twisted the guy's tie and brought him right down to the ground. After the series, Team Canada was in the Moscow airport and a Canadian reporter who had been giving Team Canada a hard time all series had a beautiful red stick that was given to him by the Russian hockey team. It was autographed by all the Russian players and coaches. John walked up to the reporter, grabbed the stick, snapped it in two and handed it back to him.

John was my GM when I went over with Team Canada to play in the World Championship in 1981. He was kind enough to let my son, Tim, come along as the stick boy. The same thing happened in the airport in Sweden after the tournament was over. This time, one of the Team Canada doctors had an autographed Russian stick. John walked over, asked to take a look at the stick and smashed it into splinters.

In 1976, John was made both general manager and coach of the New York Rangers. I was coaching Boston, and the year before John went to New York we had made the famous trade with the Rangers—Brad Park and Jean Ratelle for Phil Esposito and Carol Vadnais. My general manager, Harry Sinden, came to me and said John Ferguson had called and wondered if we wanted to trade Ken Hodge for Rick Middleton. I was not a big Ken Hodge fan, and Ken was at the end of his career. Meanwhile, Rick was a young player with a ton of talent. So I said, "In a heartbeat." The deal was done.

> **DON:** So, everybody knows Rick Middleton. Ricky was telling me a story: when he was with the New York Rangers, he came in late, as Rick was wont to do, coming in late past curfew. Now, Rick told me he was terrified of John and didn't want to get caught. So, instead of going into the lobby, he went to the underground parking and caught the elevator from there. He's in the elevator and pushes the button to the floor his room was on, and unfortunately for Rick, the elevator stopped at the lobby and you stepped in. Is that true?

> **JOHN:** Oh, I'll never forget that. I did a banquet and came back to the hotel and it was about 3 a.m. . . .

> **DON:** Rick told me it was 1 a.m. He was lying.

JOHN: So I get on the elevator and Rick sees me and puts his head down like he's a ghost and I'm not going to see him. I look at him and say, "We got a one o'clock game tomorrow." Rick looks at me and says, "Yeah, I know. I couldn't sleep, so I went for a walk." So, lo and behold, that was the start of the worst trade in history—and I made it. I was still mad about this, and we play in Vancouver and we get beat. I put Rick in the starting lineup and let him play. Ricky was a good player, but I was still mad at him. At the time, I had Phil Esposito in New York and Phil kept telling me, "Get me Ken Hodge and I'll get back to my 50-goals way." I fell for the trap. So I soon realize Ken Hodge was winding down his career. I was a rookie manager and it was an awful trade. I knew we were in trouble when Ken Hodge gave the New York Rangers' fans the bird. The gallery gods are really on Kenny; one night, we score a goal and when they announce Ken Hodge, the Ranger fans boo.

DON: So the trade was made over the summer, and on the first day of training camp, Rick skates on the ice and he looks like Porky Pig. I skate over to him and introduce myself and I look at him and say, "Geez, Ricky, I remember you in Providence and, well, you look a lot bigger now. Were you lifting weights?" Rick said, "No, Grapes, just had a good summer."

Ken Hodge only played a year and a bit with the Rangers and then was sent down to New Haven. Rick went on to play 12 more years with Boston, scoring over 440 goals and just under 900 points. So as Fergy said, one of the most lopsided trades in NHL history. Fergy called it the worst trade in history, but from Boston's point of view, it was one of the greatest trades of all time. It is all just a matter of who made the trade.

* * *

When John was coach and GM of the Rangers, they drafted a great young player who played for the Medicine Hat Tigers, Donnie Murdoch. We played them in Boston and our defenceman Mike Milbury went into the corner with Donnie. One thing led to another and they started to fight. Mike was roughing him up pretty good, and no one on the Rangers went to help Donnie. John went nuts on the Ranger bench and started throwing sticks on the ice. I remember Mike and John started jawing at each other, and I said to one of the Bruins, "I'm glad Fergy doesn't have a pair of skates or Mike would be in big trouble." I think John got thrown out of the game.

Donnie was having a great rookie season under John, but he had a bad habit of hot-dogging after a goal by standing over the goalie and dancing. In today's game, the media would say he's "just a young man expressing himself."

DON: You had a guy, Don Murdoch, should have been rookie of the year (Willi Plett of Atlanta won it that year), but at the time he was a bit of a hot dog when he scored.

JOHN: Murdoch should have been rookie of the year, but he broke his ankle. But before he broke his ankle, he could put the puck in the net. He scored five against Minnesota, and no cheap ones, but when he scored, he loved to do a little dance and give the high-fives to all the players. The word came across that the next time he scores against the Bruins and does his little dance and high-five, Grapes is going to send someone out and straighten things out. I tell Don this and to cool it, and lo and behold, the kid is not smart enough to listen to me. He scores, does the little dance and Rick Smith comes and slams him to the ice and puts his shoulder out of the socket and he misses eight games. Poor kid comes back, and the next game breaks his ankle. If he hadn't broken his ankle, he'd have won rookie of the year.

If you wanted to hot-dog back then in the "Big Boy" hockey era, you paid the price.

* * *

Years later, I was coaching Colorado and our last game was against Winnipeg, and John Ferguson was their general manager. We were two points ahead of them in the standings — unfortunately for both teams, the Jets were dead last and we were second-last in the NHL. If we lost the game, we would have the first pick in the 1980 NHL draft. But there was no way we were going to throw the game because, four years earlier, the Rockies had traded their first-round pick to Montreal for Sean Shanahan—who was not even playing in the NHL—and Ron Andruff. So, if we lost, Montreal got the first-overall pick in the 1980 NHL draft. If the Jets lost or tied, they got the number one pick. The consensus was that defenceman Dave Babych would be the first pick in that year's draft. Dave was touted as one of the best prospects in a decade.

The Jets started goalie Markus Mattsson, whose record was 5–11 with a save percentage of .887. I started Hardy Åström, whose record was 9–27 with a save percentage of .870. So it was not going to be a battle of the goalies. Before the game started, I looked up and I could see John Ferguson in his box, pacing up and down.

Hardy did his usual thing when the Jets' Dave Christian blew a 30-foot slapshot past Hardy. Then Kris Manery put one right through Hardy's legs, and we were down 2–1 after the first. Winnipeg's John Markell made it 3–1, and good guy Ron Delorme made it 3–2 going into the third. I looked and saw that John was pacing even more.

I knew, and most of the players knew, that this was probably my last period coaching in Colorado. I had been feuding with Rockies GM Ray Miron and the owners. Little did I know that it was going to be my last period of coaching in the NHL. I wanted to go out with a win, so I said to the players, "Let's go out guns blazing."

The guys didn't let me down. We poured 15 shots on

their goalie, and Mattsson stood on his head. He made four unbelievable saves, robbing Jack Valiquette, René Robert, Kevin Morrison and Lanny McDonald of sure goals. Jets won the game 3–2, so we were tied for points, but the Jets had one more win so they jumped ahead of us in the standings. It was official: Montreal got the first-over-all pick in the 1980 draft and the Jets got the second pick.

So the game was over and I looked up and saw John grabbing his phone and smashing it against the wall. He was so mad about losing the first-overall pick. One of the headlines in the Winnipeg paper was GOODBYE DAVID BABYCH.

That year was one of the most controversial drafts in NHL history. The draft was held in Montreal, and the Canadiens held the first pick. And by this time, it looked like John Ferguson and the Jets were going to get Dave Babych after all. There was a great little player playing for the Montreal Junior Canadiens in the Quebec Major Junior Hockey League named Denis Savard. Denis was from Pointe Gatineau, Quebec, and he was tearing up the league. In three seasons with the Montreal juniors, he had 147 goals and over 450 points. It was a shoo-in that the Canadiens were going to take Savard. He was French, fast like a little water bug and could score a ton of goals. The Forum was packed with Montreal fans just waiting to hear Canadiens general manager Irving Grundman call out Denis Savard's name.

Instead of Savard, the Canadiens picked Doug Wickenheiser, a centre for the Regina Pats. Now, Doug was no slouch in junior. In his last season of junior hockey with the Pats, he scored 89 goals and had 170 points and

100 minutes in penalties. But for Montreal to pass over a young French-Canadian player was a big mistake. The fans went nuts.

I felt bad for Doug. The Montreal fans and press never forgave the Canadiens for not taking Denis. Doug ended up playing 556 games, scoring 111 goals and over 276 points, while Denis played 1,196 games, scored 473 goals and 1,338 points.

So that year, John Ferguson got the player he wanted, Dave Babych, who went on to play six years with the Jets and 22 seasons in the NHL.

I got fired.

BLUE

Blue and Eric Lindros meet at one of the Grapevine Pubs.

I ALWAYS HAD DOGS WHEN I was growing up in Kingston. I had a Labrador named Dungeon and an English bulldog named Topper. When I started playing pro hockey, Rose and I moved around 32 times, so there was no way we could have had one—it would not have been fair to the dog, moving so much. In 1962, we settled down in Rochester, New York, and bought a house. We decided to get a dog, and Rose wanted a small dog. So we got a miniature poodle named Ginger, and after Ginger we had a Maltese named Casper.

Rose had gotten the dogs she wanted, and now it was my turn to get a dog that *I* wanted. I had always wanted an English bull terrier. Bull terriers were bred for fighting in the pits back in the 1800s and quickly earned the nickname "The White Cavalier" for their courage in the pits. At the time, the most famous English bull terrier had been Willie, General George Patton's dog. Patton had bull terriers for most of his life since the end of World War I. John Steinbeck and American president Woodrow Wilson also had bull terriers.

The bull terrier was not overly popular back in the early '70s. You had to go to a breeder, so the puppies were fairly expensive, and Rose and I had to watch our spending. Someone told me about a woman just outside New York who bred bull terriers for show dogs. I called her and she said she had some puppies for sale, so Cindy, Tim, Rose and I jumped into my '64 Pontiac and headed for Long Island. Somehow we found the house after driving through New York City and we pulled into the driveway. As we were getting out of the car, a huge head peeked through the curtains in the window. It was a bull terrier named Gus. Gus was a bit of a freak because he was twice the size of a normal bull terrier.

Rose said, "Oh my God, I hope they are all not that big."

We got into the house, where Gus had ripped open a large bag of dog food and spilled it all over the place. Again, Rose was not impressed. The breeder took us outside, where most of the dogs were in kennels except for one little white pup playing with her children. I asked about the pup, and she said they had just gotten her a few weeks ago. Her husband had gone to pick the puppy out of a litter. He had gone at night and didn't notice that she had two blue eyes, the worst trait a bull terrier could have. They didn't know what they were going to do with it because of the blue eyes—they were thinking of putting the pup down. They didn't want to put her down because she had a great personality, and her children loved the pup.

I said, "We'll take her."

The woman agreed on one condition: that we got the dog fixed so she could never have puppies. Cindy named her Blue because of her eyes, and we got back into the '64 Pontiac and headed home. That night, we ran into a terrible storm and had to stay overnight in a cheap motel. The four of us were in one room with our beautiful new dog, Blue.

That was the summer of 1971, and I was at the lowest point in my life. I'd just been laid off from Ridge Construction and I couldn't even get a job sweeping floors. The day we got Blue, my luck started to turn around. Not being able to find a job, I got on my knees and asked the Lord what I was going to do to feed my family, and a voice as clear as a bell told me to make a comeback with the Rochester Americans. I went from picking up Blue that summer to coaching the Rochester Americans six months later. I was coaching Bobby Orr three years after that.

* * *

When we got home from picking up Blue, I realized we had a bit of a problem. We had not had a dog in a while, and though the backyard was fenced in, there was no door from the house to the backyard—only a couple of windows. So I built a ramp leading to one of the windows, and Blue soon learned that when she had to go outside, she would go to the window and we'd open it and lift her up, and down the ramp she'd go to the backyard. Now, many people will tell you that bull terriers are not that smart of a dog, but Blue must have been an exception.

When you get a bull terrier, you soon realize that they are not only the "White Cavalier" of the dog world, but they are also the athletes of the canine kingdom. They are fast, impervious to pain and carved out of rock-solid muscle. They also have personality plus. They are clown-ish, love to be mischievous and are very headstrong. Many dog books say they can be hard of hearing, but they hear you; they just don't listen to you all the time. They are like Terry O'Reilly: very docile unless you rile them up—then look out.

When Blue was a pup, she was walking on a leash when she saw a cat and went up to play with it. The cat scratched her pretty good. From that day, any cat or squirrel that crossed her path had better look out. A few months later, days after Blue had an operation, she saw a cat in our neighbour's yard. In the blink of an eye, she climbed a four-foot-high chain-link fence, fell on a bunch of hockey sticks being used as tomato stakes and took after the cat. If the cat had gone behind a brick wall, Blue would have gone through the brick wall to get at it. That was when I realized how much of an athletic and intense dog she was, and that was exactly how I wanted my teams to play.

Tim had a bunch of pucks in the backyard, and Blue's jaws were so strong that she would chew them to pieces in a matter of minutes. I once caught her chewing a puck and tried to take it off her, and I couldn't make her let go, no matter how hard I pulled. I literally picked her up off the ground and she didn't let go. After finally wrestling the puck out of her mouth, I took the half-chewed puck down to the dressing room the next day. I showed it to the players and said, "When Blue was chewing the puck, she was in a frenzy. This is how I want you to play, in a frenzy."

That's how some reporters described the Bruins—that they played in a frenzy.

Another thing we quickly learned about bull terriers is that you don't fool around with them or tease them, because they will always remember. One day, Blue was all riled up and Cindy kept saying, "Who's that?" That became Blue's cue word to start barking and growling. Later, Rose was at home alone and a seedy-looking man came to the door and said he needed to read the gas meter, which was in the basement. The guy looked like a creep and didn't have a uniform or official ID and was acting kind of aggressive.

Rose told the guy to wait, and then she got Blue and said, "Who's that?" Blue went nuts, barking and growling. When she got into that state, she'd swell up to twice her size.

The guy's face went white and he said, "That's okay. I'll come back later." He never came back, and there is no doubt that Blue saved Rose that day.

The one thing Blue didn't like was splashing water. I don't know how that came about, but anytime Blue saw a hose running, she'd grab it and start to shake it like a rag doll. In Rochester, we had an above-ground pool with a small raised deck. When we went swimming, Blue would start barking and run around the pool. Rose made me put up a gate so Blue couldn't get up on the deck.

One day, Rose asked me if I thought Blue would bite me if she was on the deck when I jumped into the pool. I didn't think she would, so Blue came up on the deck and I jumped in. Blue didn't bite me, but she misjudged her timing and took a little nip out of my thigh accidentally. Rose said it looked like a harpooned whale as the blood spread out in the water. What made things worse was that I had just put chlorine in the pool and it really stung. I got out of the pool, and Blue knew she'd made a mistake and ran down and went under a small deck. I got a hockey stick, crawled underneath the deck and gave her a good swat with the stick. She let me get away with it once, and a second time, and then she turned and grabbed the stick and I couldn't pull it out of her mouth. She was growling as if to say, "Okay, that's enough." I thought to myself that I was under this deck and she was telling me to back off, so I'd better get out of there.

Blue was an affectionate dog. She was always excited to see me when I came home. Only a driveway separated the side door to our house from our neighbour's window. One day, our neighbour came over and said to Rose, "Gee, Rose, I didn't know Don was so affectionate."

Rose said, "What are you talking about?"

The neighbor said, "I don't mean to pry, but I can hear him through our window when he comes home. He keeps telling you how he misses you and how sweet you are."

Rose said, "He's talking to the dog."

That's the one great thing about dogs: they don't care if you win or lose the game, they're just happy to see you come home.

* * *

Every once in a while, I would take Blue down to the Rochester War Memorial for a practice or when a team picture was being taken. In the dressing room, the players started to tease her with a goalie mask and sticks. During practice, I didn't realize that she'd gotten out of the dressing room and was trying to get at the players on the ice by biting the wire fence.

In the War Memorial, the visitors' dressing room was in the basement and the team had to walk up two flights of stairs to get to the rink. Blue was out running around, and the Richmond Robins' goalie was leading his team up the stairs for a morning skate. Blue saw the mask and stood at the top of the stairs, barking and growling at the goalie. He stopped and tried waving his stick at her, and she grabbed it. He was yelling for help and I came and put Blue back in the dressing room.

That year, when we took the team picture, winger Rod Graham brought down his Doberman named Amerk and I brought Blue down. We took a team photo with them, and then put Amerk and Blue in the dressing room while we practised. Both of them started to play and run around the dressing room. Our trainer, Nate, was trapped in a back room and was too afraid to try and get out the door. By the time practice was over, they had totally destroyed the place.

All the players' clothes were on the floor, and they had knocked over the trash can and the table with all the tape and stuff. It was funny to come in the dressing room after practice and see the mess the dogs had made of the place.

* * *

It was when I went to Boston that Blue started to become famous. I was sitting in my office and one of the Boston newspaper reporters asked who was playing goal that night. For some reason, I said, "Well, I talked it over with Blue and she says to start Cheevers."

The reporters got a big kick out of it and played up that "Cherry's dog picks starting goalie." We won the game, and the next day the reporters came in and said, "Okay, Grapes, who does Blue say should play goal tonight?"

I started talking about Blue and telling the press how I wanted the Bruins to play like Blue, full out and with an attitude. Blue became more and more popular and became a favourite subject for many sports cartoons in the paper and even a TV commercial for the Bruins. When Bruins fans came up for an autograph, most of them were nervous and didn't know what to say, but soon almost all of them would ask, "How's Blue?" and I would always say, "She can't be here but she sends her love." They would start talking about their dogs—it's a great ice-breaker asking someone how their dog is doing. It got to the point where there was a petition to get a bull terrier to replace the Boston terrier as the Massachusetts state dog. In the petition, it said that the fighting, never-quit

spirit of a bull terrier like Blue was more representative of
the Boston people than the Boston terrier, which is just
conveniently named after the city of Boston.

Blue's popularity helped save the day for me one summer.
Behind our house in North Andover was a large state forest
where I would take Blue for walks. On a summer day, I took
her for a walk and we went very far back into the forest,
which was thousands of acres. There were no trails or
paths, and the forest was so untouched that Tim found
arrowheads just lying on the ground when he went into
the woods with his friends. Blue and I must have walked
for over an hour when we came to an old, abandoned
mill, and by it was a beautiful stream. I laid down to close
my eyes for a minute, and I woke up a good half hour later.
When I woke up, I didn't know where I was for a minute.
When I got my bearings, I kind of knew which way was
home, but there were no paths, trails or markers. Just trees.
I started walking the way I thought was home, and after
about a half hour we came back to the mill. I had been
walking in circles. It was getting dark and I was getting a
little nervous.

Blue was looking at me, saying, "Come on, dummy, let's
go home."

I found an old piece of rope in the mill and tied it
around Blue because it was getting dark quickly and I
didn't want to lose her in the dark. We walked for about
another hour when I could hear the sound of traffic. In
about 15 minutes, we came to Highway 114, about 10 miles
from home. I started walking along the road when a car of
young guys drove past and then put on the brakes.

They backed up, rolled down the window and said, "Hey, Don Cherry, want a ride?"

I played it cool, as if Blue and I were just out for a stroll, but boy, was I glad they stopped. Blue and I hopped in and I said, "Glad you guys recognized me."

They laughed and said, "Well, to tell you the truth, we recognized Blue first."

Rose was out front when the guys pulled in the driveway. When they drove off, she asked, "Who are those guys and where have you been all this time?"

Again I played it cool and said, "Blue and I went for a walk and those guys are some fans that drove us home."

I used to take Blue for long walks in the winter during the season. In the forest behind the house was an old, abandoned railroad track, and Blue and I would take walks there for hours. With just the two of us in the middle of the woods, all alone, that was the time I would talk out loud to Blue about the Bruins and what was going on with the team. In the 1979 semifinals against Montreal, we lost the first two games at the Forum. Our goalie, Gerry Cheevers, played okay, but I needed to shake things up. While taking a walk with Blue and talking to her I weighed putting Gilles Gilbert in goal. Now, Gilbert and I didn't get along and he had not played in over a month. But while talking to Blue, I looked at it a different way. He was French and loved to play against Montreal in front of his family, and his contract was up at the end of the year, so he would be playing for a new contract. I remember saying, "Well, Blue, we're not winning the way things are going now, so I'm going with Gilbert." Blue agreed. I announced that Gilbert was playing Game 3, we won 2–1, and Gilbert was picked as the game's first star. He won Game 4 in overtime and went on to take Montreal to Game 7, where we lost in overtime. After the game, one of the reporters told me, "If you played Gilbert sooner, you would have won the series." If only I had taken Blue for a walk sooner.

You could take her for a walk, but you also had to exercise her to get out all that energy. Blue was a real throwback as bull terriers go. She was a little leggier than the bull terrier of the day, and she was faster and more athletic than modern-day bull terriers, and that's saying something. You had to exercise her once or twice a day or she'd be in a bad mood. In our house in North Andover, Massachusetts, we had a big front yard. I would throw a tennis ball to Blue to burn off all that energy. I would get lost in thought about the team and lose track of time. By the time I snapped out of it, my shoulder was sore and Blue's paws were bleeding. Rose would always get mad because I'd come into the house after throwing the ball to Blue and she'd be tracking blood all over the floor. She'd chase that ball for hours, and that's how she got so muscular. When you petted her, it was like petting a horse. It got to the point where, to wear her out, I had to get a tennis racquet to hit the ball because my shoulder wouldn't hold out throwing a tennis ball that long.

I kept telling the players in all seriousness that this was the attitude that I wanted the players to play with at all times. I have to say that in Rochester and Boston, we did play with Blue's attitude. Stan Jonathan brought his family down to the dressing room one morning. I went into my office and they were watching Stan's fight on the video. Stan introduced me to his father and I said, "Mr. Jonathan, your son reminds me of my dog, Blue." Stan's father looked at me kind of strange, and Stan had to explain to him that it was my highest form of praise.

I know it's hard to believe that, during the summer, the players came over to our house to play tennis and go for a swim. Peter McNab was our 40-goal scorer and he had two lovely golden retrievers, and Peter was the Bruins' golden retriever. I always told Peter that even a team of bull terriers needed a couple of golden retrievers.

Peter came to our house one summer day and played some tennis and then went for a swim. Our pool got full sun from sunup till sundown and the water was very warm. Peter was swimming laps after his game of tennis and got out of the pool and went over to the water hose. Peter said the water was so warm that he needed to cool off after swimming the laps. He turned on the hose and Blue took notice. She went full speed towards Peter.

I yelled, "Peter, drop the hose!" Peter looked up and saw Blue in full fury coming at him, and he dropped the hose just in the nick of time as Blue jumped and grabbed the hose and started to tear into it. Peter looked shocked. I'm glad he dropped the hose in time; it would have been hard to explain to Harry that Blue took out our 40-goal scorer.

* * *

I only brought Blue down to Boston Garden a few times. Once was for a TV commercial and a photo shoot in the

Bruins dressing room with Gary Doak, Rick Smith and Gerry Cheevers' sweaters and Gilles Gilbert's mask in the background. The other time was for the team photo. All the Bruins were in place to take the team picture. Blue was on the Bruins bench, and somehow the bench door closed. I called Blue, and she didn't want to jump over the boards. Instead, she took off under the stands. All the players laughed.

Blue found her way under the stands to the other side of the ice, where the door to the visitors' bench was open, and ran on the ice. I picked her up and tried to settle her down for the picture. Harry Sinden was sitting beside me, and for some reason, Blue started to growl at Harry. Harry looked a little uncomfortable with Blue only a few feet from him, growling. Someone snapped a picture and put it in one of the papers with the headline BRUINS GOING TO THE DOGS. Harry was not amused.

* * *

In 1979, I went to Denver and coached the Colorado Rockies. Blue didn't like Denver for many reasons, but the main one was the altitude. Denver is a mile above sea level, and the altitude affected her, so she couldn't go for long walks. One morning, I brought Blue down for the Rockies' morning skate. While I was on the ice, I put Blue in the office and taped a sign on the door that read, "Stay out. Blue is in here." A reporter from Hartford ignored my sign and went into my office and started looking at things on my desk. Blue came flying out from under my desk and grabbed his foot and started shaking it. We could hear him screaming, and I ran into my office and pulled Blue off him. He was so upset and scared that we had to take him into the trainer's room and have him lie down on a medical table. Later, when he recovered, he said to me, "Grapes, that teaches me a lesson. I am going to start to pay attention to signs on doors."

In 1982, we moved to Mississauga, Ontario, and Blue was a new dog. The altitude was close to what it was in Boston and she looked five years younger. We bought a house with a large field across the street so I could take Blue for walks. She was around eleven years old and still in great shape. After coming home from a taping of a *Grapevine* show, I let Blue out in our backyard. After a few minutes, Rose and I started to smell a skunk. Then the smell became unbearable. I went out to get Blue, and I couldn't find her, but I could hear her growling and the smell of skunk brought tears to my eyes. I found her with a huge male skunk's head in her mouth. They had fought for about five minutes and they had fallen into a window well. The skunk was spraying Blue so much that it was dripping off her. The smell was so powerful it stopped smelling like skunk and became something even stronger. Blue was shaking her head and the skunk just kept spraying her.

I grabbed Blue, she let go of the skunk to get a better grip, and I pulled her out of the window well. The skunk just lay there, and Blue was trying to get back at her opponent. The skunk spray had soaked Blue so much it looked like someone had poured a bucket of water on her. Rose came out with some newspapers and I started to wipe the skunk spray off her. I was just throwing the newspapers around while trying to get the skunk spray off her and away from her eyes. I looked over my shoulder and thought I saw the skunk with its tail in the air. Blue saw it too, and judging by the look on her face, it was as if she was saying, "All right, you son of a bitch, that was round one." She took off after it. Luckily, it was just a newspaper being blown around by the wind. I could have kissed her.

We brought her into the house and put her in a washtub. We poured tomato juice on her, but nothing could get that smell off her. Nothing worked, and Blue just started drinking the tomato juice. Years later, when she got wet, you could still smell skunk.

I went to the basement and checked the window that Blue and the skunk were fighting in, and the screen had melted away from the skunk spray. The skunk was alive and was trying to get at me through the window. I went outside, got a split rail from a fence, and put it down the window well, and the next morning the skunk was gone. The smell was so strong that it not only melted the window screen, but it also started to peel the paint off a metal door.

* * *

Blue truly did show me how I wanted my players to play, and she also showed me how I needed to act on television. The one thing Blue showed me was that it's all about attitude. I have a cottage at Wolfe Island across from Kingston,

Ontario. When we first got the place, a great guy named Dugan Collins owned a cottage down the road. Dugan was from Rochester, New York, and he and his family had four dogs, mostly Labs. I was taking Blue for a walk and these four big Labs came charging for her. Blue just kept walking and sniffing around. When the four dogs got closer, Blue just looked at them and sauntered towards them. The four dogs stopped in their tracks and backed off. It was just Blue's attitude that intimidated those dogs.

One day, unbeknownst to me, Dugan had let a friend of his stay at the cottage, and he had two huge Great Danes. One was a Harlequin and had to be over a hundred pounds; the other one was pure black, with grey eyes and cropped ears. It was one of the scariest-looking dogs I've ever seen. It looked like a hellhound. It was over a hundred pounds too. I let Blue out—she weighed about 40 pounds—and these two monsters were in our yard. My heart was in my mouth; it looked like they could have swallowed Blue whole, and they were looking for trouble. But despite not even coming up to their chests in height, Blue walked right up to them and started bumping into them. The two big Great Danes didn't know what to do. Blue's tail was straight up in the air, and you could feel the vibes she was giving off as if she was saying, "Go ahead, try something. I dare you." She was just like Stan Jonathan.

The Great Danes started to back off and then turned tail and ran home. It was all attitude that made those two monsters back down.

When I go on "Coach's Corner," it's all about attitude. On television, you have to be confident, or the viewers will see right through you. You have to have confidence and the attitude that what you say is right and you know what you're talking about. That encounter between Blue and those two Great Danes taught me that.

* * *

I'll end this with one of my favourite stories about Blue. In the old Boston Garden, I was walking to the dressing room. Wayne Cashman came up to me and said, "What's going on, Grapes? You look down."

I said, "Cash, I have bad news. Blue bit Cindy and she had to get stitches."

Cash just shook his head. "Well, that's it, Grapes. It's over. You have to get rid of her."

I said, "Yeah. And I liked Cindy."

THE LIFE OF A PLAYER, COACH & TV PERSONALITY

Shooting a cold open for the *Grapevine* show.
Somebody stole that picture during the last night of taping.
Needless to say I was a little upset.

I AM OFTEN ASKED QUESTIONS LIKE: How did I get started in hockey? What is the life of a junior hockey player like? What is the life of a professional hockey player like? What is the life of a general manager and a coach like? What is the life of a radio and television commentator like?

Well, when I was young, every night I got on my knees and said my prayers, and in those prayers, I would ask God to make me a hockey player. Unfortunately, I forgot to say an *NHL* hockey player. The Lord did answer my prayers, and I went from minor hockey to junior hockey to pro hockey.

I have to say that becoming a GM, coach and television commentator was driven by the need to feed my family.

After I retired from hockey, I was working at Ridge Construction in Rochester, New York. One of my best friends was Whitey Smith, and he was my foreman. We'd all heard that layoffs were coming, and after one day at work they called everybody into a room and started saying thanks for all our work for the company. They called my name and Whitey was in tears. Management had told Whitey I was safe, but they laid me off anyway. After that, I couldn't get a job.

As I am writing this, I realize that the greatest motivator for any job, the greatest motivator for success, is hunger. After hockey, I was humiliated—it's hard to say, but true. I was a good construction worker with a pick and shovel and a jackhammer. After I was laid off, I couldn't get a job in construction, so I tried to sell cars. I soon became the world's worst car salesman. I got hired at Valley Cadillac in Rochester. I was not cut out to be in sales. One day, a guy came in and asked about a car. I gave him the pitch and he said, "All you car salesmen are alike."

I asked him what he'd said, and he told me again: "All you car salesmen are alike."

I grabbed him by the collar and pinned him against the wall, daring him to say it again.

I had no choice but to go back to hockey, directed by the Lord.

I went back to try out for the Amerks. The trainer of the club humiliated me when training camp started. He put me in the room with the rookies and walk-ons. Three years earlier, I was the captain of the Amerks when we won the Calder Cup. When I made my comeback, the trainer gave me the worst gloves he could find—gloves with large holes in them.

I found out it was a cruel world, something I'd never learned in hockey. I was like most hockey players—how did I think it was never going to end? Some guys did prepare for the end of hockey, like my defence partner Darryl Sly. He went to college and was preparing for the future. He went on to open some car dealerships in Collingwood, Ontario, and became very successful. After 18 years of hockey, I had no education, no career, no trade and no job. It was a tough go. The burning desire of the humiliation drove me.

When I was offered the job as coach of the Rochester Americans, I said, "Just give me a chance." Anybody who is out of a job knows what I mean. Just take the Vegas Golden Knights. The players on that team were told that they weren't wanted. The teams they played on said to the Knights, "Go ahead. You can have that guy. We don't need him." When those players were told they were not going to be protected by the clubs they were on and that Vegas could draft them, they were humiliated.

When they got to Vegas, they were hungry and had something to prove to their old clubs and to the NHL. It's us against the world. Look at Golden Knights coach Gerard Gallant. He's played over 615 NHL games and has been coaching for 18 years in the IHL, AHL, QMJHL and NHL. In 2016–17, Gerard was coaching the Florida Panthers. It was his third year in Florida, and the team was doing pretty good for an organization that was rebuilding. The team had been playing well, winning five of its past seven games. Some new owners who didn't know a thing about hockey had bought the team. Florida was playing in Carolina and lost 3–2, and then the Panthers fired Gerard right after the game. It was one of the worst handlings of a coach being fired in the history of the NHL. There was a picture in the paper of Gerard getting into a cab from the hotel. He had to get his bags from the team bus—with the players sitting in the bus, ready to go back to the hotel—and catch a cab to the airport.

I went on "Coach's Corner" and said, "I've been involved in hockey a long time. I've seen some bad firings. I've been fired myself. I thought in Colorado it was rather bad. I have never seen anything like this. This is the worst firing in the history of the NHL. They fire the guy after the game; the players are sitting on the bus. He has to grab his bags and get a cab. There was a great headline I saw in the paper, DUMPED AT THE CURB."

Panthers management humiliated Gerard. When Vegas' GM, George McPhee, hired Gerard, I said it was a great move. Gallant wanted a chance to show the world that the Panthers had made a mistake. The players McPhee drafted in the expansion draft wanted a chance to show the world that teams giving up on them were a mistake. Vegas finished first in their division and fifth overall in the NHL, the greatest expansion team in NHL history, and in my mind the biggest story in sports right now. As I write this, they're in the Stanley Cup finals against Washington. The Vegas Golden Knights have shown that nothing can motivate like hunger, like the burning desire to bounce back from a humiliating experience.

My Bruins always played hungrily. It was us against the world again. I remember doing a press conference, and I took a hockey magazine called *Goal* that was as big as the *Hockey News* back then and said to the press, "How come the Bruins are never on the cover of *Goal* magazine? You know why? The press and the league don't like the Bruins." And the funny thing was, we were never on the cover! It was always us against the world, an attitude that drove us to prove the world wrong.

Sometimes, good players lose their hunger. How many times has a good player signed a contract for big dough and then become just a mediocre player? They sign for big dough and they lose their hunger. They think, "I am making big dough now, I don't want to get hurt, so I'll go through the motions." The trick to being successful is staying hungry, but that's not easy.

There is a great story about Jack Dempsey, the world heavyweight boxing champion, who was living the good life. In September of 1926, he fought a boxer named Gene Tunney who was a heavy underdog in the fight. Jack lost the bout and his title. After the fight, Jack's wife asked how he could lose his title to a guy like that. Jack smiled and shook his head and said, "Honey, it's tough to get up at 4:30 in the morning and run 10 miles in silk shorts."

In other words, Jack had lost his hunger.

* * *

I started to write this chapter about a day in the life of a hockey player, coach and television guy, and I got carried away by talking about how I started coaching because of my hunger to feed my family and the humiliation I went through when I was making a comeback.

Okay, back to the life of a player.

I started my hockey life in junior. Back when I was a junior player, we didn't go into a draft like they do today. The NHL teams would sign you to a contract, or a C form, as it was called. The Bruins signed me and I went to their rookie camp in Barrie, Ontario. I remember it like it was yesterday: the Bruins had all the rookies on the ice and one of the Bruins management was in the stands, talking, letting us know what was expected of us. He went on to say, "I know you guys skated yesterday. Do any of you guys have sore muscles?" Some wise guy standing next to me yelled out, "Yeah, the love muscle." I almost fainted because the Bruins boss looked over towards me and I was afraid that he thought I had said it. I still remember what the wise guy looked like. He was gone the next day.

I made the Barrie Flyers the next year, and then I was lent to the Windsor Spitfires. That year, I went to school. We were at school till 2:30, and then we would go and have practice. I remember the school was just a few blocks away from the rink. I was out in the schoolyard during gym class. We had to wear these funny shorts, and I looked up and saw a bunch of my teammates from Windsor walking to the rink. I said, "Please God, don't let them see me." They would have made fun of me all year.

The next year, I quit school, and that was a big mistake. When I told my mom on the phone that I had quit school, she started to cry.

If you didn't go to school, you had to have a job. I didn't have one, so I had to report to the bus station at eight o'clock every morning and sweep out the buses. You'd think I would have clued in that this was the life I was heading for if I didn't get an education, but I only had pro hockey on my mind.

So, my life in junior hockey was work in the morning, practice and/or game, then back to the billet for a 10 p.m. curfew.

In pro, it was a little different. On the day of a game, it was up at 8 a.m., practice at 10 a.m. and then lunch. And after lunch, a nap. Hockey players always have to have a nap. That way, when a player is traded and he has to travel and get to his new team's game, he'll always say afterward, "It was a crazy day for me, and I didn't get to have my nap." When you see players walking into the rink before the game on *Hockey Night in Canada*, they always look a little dopey, like they just got up. That's because they *have* just gotten up from a nap. That's the reason they're carrying a coffee as they walk into the rink—to help them wake up.

Now, I can only speak for the AHL. When we were on the road, we'd get back on the bus after the game and head to the next city, and naturally, we'd have some pops on the bus. We were always thirsty after the game because we were not allowed to drink during a game. Back then, they thought if you drank water, you'd get a cramp or you'd be bloated. So, after the game, we'd down that first pop pretty quick. Some of the guys would go to the back of the bus and start to play cards. Others would settle down and read or fall asleep. Sometimes we'd stop on the way to the next city and get something to eat. When I played in Hershey, we'd always play a joke on our trainer, Scotty Alexander. One of the players would go into the restaurant before Scotty and point him out to the waitress and tell her to serve him last, no matter what. So all the players would be sitting down in a small diner that was almost empty, in the middle of the night, and the waitress would be serving everybody but Scotty and he'd be steaming mad.

Sometimes, we'd head straight to the next city we were playing in; other times, we'd stop and get a motel in the middle of the night. I didn't like that, and I never did it when I coached. We'd get off the bus half asleep and head into these motel rooms that were cold and damp and it felt like no one had been in the rooms for months. We'd just get to sleep, and then we'd have to get up and get back on the bus and finish the trip. Most times, we were woken up by the starting of the engine in the bus, which we called the iron lung. Sometimes, the bus driver would need to put ether in the engine to get it going. I don't know why we did this. We never got a good sleep, we were always tired, and we'd have no breakfast. It was insanity. When I became a coach, we always drove straight through to the city we were playing in.

We'd arrive in the city, check into the hotel, and we'd have our team pre-game lunch. We'd all sit together and we'd all have the same thing: steaks. Today, all the players eat pasta. After the meal, we'd all head up to our rooms for our pre-game nap with our little cups of vanilla ice cream. I can still see all the guys in the elevator, going to the rooms, eating ice cream with chocolate sauce. We'd head down to the lobby, get on the bus and head to the rink. We'd play the game and it would start all over again. Life was great.

Things were different when I became the coach and general manager in Rochester. I went and got players that were heading to the EHL. They were hungry like a wolf, just like me. Like I said, these guys wanted to prove to the world that they were good hockey players. It was soon "us against the world."

Being a GM was different than being a coach or a player. I had to be in the office every day. In Rochester, I had a great assistant GM named John DenHamer. I took care of all the hockey stuff and John dealt with the business of running a hockey team, because I was still thinking like a player.

And like I said, when we were on the road, I hated stopping halfway and going to those cold, clammy motels. So I would pack the bus with beer and sandwiches and tell the players we were going all the way to the next city. They loved it, even though we'd get into the city about 4 a.m. The owners liked it too, because we'd save money on hotels.

One difference between being a coach and being a player was the stress level. You'd go to bed and the last thing you'd be thinking about was the next game. You'd get up in the morning and the first thing you'd think about was the next game. You were constantly thinking about the team and the games.

Coaching in the NHL was different, too. In Boston, there were no more buses; we took charter flights from city to city. We had steak dinners and drinks on the plane. But a funny thing happened in my second year of coaching Boston. We stopped taking charter flights and started flying commercial, so that the owners could save money. I was not too happy at first, and then I realized it turned out to be the best thing ever, because we started to come together as a team. On the road, we'd finish the game and if we chartered out, we'd head straight to the airport. But when we flew commercial, we would have to catch a flight early the next morning. So, as a team, we'd go out to a bar and have some pops. We came together as a team. Some might say we bonded as a team. (I hate that word *bonded*.)

The amount of stress that came with coaching in Boston was another difference from the AHL. In my third year, I had such a bad back that I could hardly stand. Now, I couldn't call Harry and say, "Harry, my back hurts. I can't make the game." So I had to get Rose to help me put my pants on, then tie my shoes and then drive me down to Boston Garden. I got to the game, and when I went behind the bench, I had to stand in one spot. The guys who bought tickets right behind where I was standing couldn't see a thing, and they kept banging on the glass for me to move. I couldn't move, and were they pissed.

My back hurt because of stress. Like I said, the last thing I would think of before I went to bed was the next game, and the first thing I would think of when I got up was the next game. I became a Rolaids junkie. I'd eat them like candy. When I ran out, I was in a panic. Again, all because of stress. But life was a ball in Boston, stress or no stress.

Well, I went to Colorado and it didn't go so good. Stayed for one year, and then I was back in Toronto, and thank goodness the Emmy Award–winning executive producer of *Hockey Night in Canada,* Ralph Mellanby, liked me and put me on the telecast. People ask me what I do on Saturday to get ready for "Coach's Corner." I have to say that my routine has not changed that much from when I was a player. I get up in the morning and have my breakfast, and then around 9:30 a.m., Ron calls and we go over what we are going to talk about that night. I don't know why we do this, because once we start "Coach's Corner," we don't often stick to the script. That phone call is like a morning skate. Ron and I are getting ready for "Coach's Corner" that night.

Then, for lunch, I have my steak dinner, just like when I was playing. After lunch, I have my nap, just like the players, and then it's off to the arena. I arrive about 5:30 p.m.

I like to go on "Coach's Corner" on an empty stomach. I eat my lunch at 1 p.m. and the show airs around 7:45 p.m., and I don't eat anything until I get home. When I am in the studio or on the road in the press room, I see guys eating an hour or so before they go on the air. I don't know how they do that; I have to have an empty stomach and three cups of coffee before I go on "Coach's Corner." When you see the players walking into the rink before the game, they are all drinking coffee, just like I have to have coffee before "Coach's Corner."

The head of Sportsnet, my boss, is Scott Moore. Scott was once asked, "How long will Don Cherry be on *Hockey Night in Canada?*" Scott replied, "Don has been a good horse for us, and when we think he's finished, we'll just shoot him." Scott was just joking, I think.

Just like the hockey players say, "You're only as good as your last shift," I guess you are only as good as your last segment on television. People ask me how long I am going to stay on "Coach's Corner." I know the end is coming, but not yet. I'll know when to leave. When I go on the "Coach's Corner" set and I don't feel those butterflies in my stomach and I'm not excited to go on, it will be time to move on.

But until then, I'll stay on and I'll stay hungry.

2018 PLAYOFFS AND BEYOND

Ron and me in Winnipeg before Game 2 of the Jets vs. Knights semifinals.

TO VEGAS AND BACK

IT'S THE FIRST ROUND OF THE 2018 Stanley Cup playoffs, and Toronto is playing Boston. I got into some hot water for saying I was rooting for Boston, but why wouldn't I? I became part of their organization when I was 15 years old. Don't get me wrong; someday, I'd like to see the Leafs win the Cup for their fans. I'd like to see that "fine broth of a lad," Brendan Shanahan, be the one to bring a Cup home. And when the Leafs go deep in the playoffs, it's great for the ratings. When I'm not cheering for Boston, of course I'm rooting for the Leafs.

I can see that Leafs superstar Auston Matthews is in a bit of a funk. I know he's not happy with his ice time—he's only getting 17 and a half minutes a game. Mike Babcock's trying to keep him away from Bruins defenceman Zdeno Chára, who still plays close to 25 minutes a game. I'm not knocking Babcock, but when I was a coach, I never wanted my players to have a negative thought. I don't like telling any player, "You're not good enough to play against that guy." If I were in Babcock's place, I would play Matthews against Chára. Matter of fact, I'd double-shift him.

You've always got to focus on the positive. During the '79 semifinals, *Hockey Night in Canada* asked me, "How are you going to handle the Montreal Canadiens?"

I answered, "You got it all wrong. The question is 'How is Montreal going to handle the Boston Bruins?'" Always be positive.

The Leafs get beat out by Boston in seven games. Freddy Andersen has played well, so it isn't his fault.

* * *

Usually, during the playoffs, we do "Coach's Corner" from the studios in Toronto. In the third round, with the Jets the only Canadian team left, Ron and I are going to go to Winnipeg for the first two games against Las Vegas. The Jets have everything going for them—good goalie, good defence and tough forwards. But something throws Winnipeg off. I like Dustin Byfuglien; he's a force on the ice. But he scores a goal in Game 1 and does a little dance. I get a bad feeling when I see something like that.

I had the same feeling back in 1993, when the Leafs were in the semifinals against the LA Kings. The winner was to go on and meet the Montreal Canadiens in the final. The Leafs were up 3–2 in games going into Game 6 in LA. Ron and I were at the morning skate, and I turned to him and said, "The Leafs are not winning this series."

Ron said, "Why would you say that? The Leafs only have to win one out of the next two."

It was just a feeling, a vibe I was getting. Little did I know that in that game, Wayne Gretzky would high-stick Doug Gilmour and cut him. Back then, if you drew blood, it was an automatic five-minute major. Referee Kerry Fraser missed the call. It's funny: all the players saw the high stick, three million *Hockey Night in Canada* viewers saw the high stick, the 18,000 fans at the Forum saw the high stick, but Kerry Fraser and the two linesmen missed it. To make matters worse, Fraser called a chintzy boarding call on the Leafs' Glenn Anderson with 13 seconds left in the third period with the score tied 4–4. The Kings scored on the power play at 1:40 of the overtime, and guess who got the goal? Gretzky.

Game 7 was at Maple Leaf Gardens, and the Kings won 5–4 and moved on to the finals. Gretzky said it was his best game ever—he scored a hat trick and got an assist. I remember he was behind the Leafs net in the third period and he banked the puck off of Dave Ellett's skate, past Félix Potvin for the winner. It wasn't a lucky bounce. He did it on purpose.

Winnipeg is the best team left in the playoffs, but Vegas goalie Marc-André Fleury is killing them in the semifinals. I keep saying on "Coach's Corner" that the Jets have to start bugging him, getting in front of him, because he's seeing too many shots. After Game 3, Fleury tells Scott

Oake that the players are doing a great job in front of him "and I am seeing everything."

After the first game against Winnipeg—a 4–2 loss—Fleury has at least a .945 save percentage in every game. In the clinching Game 5, he has a .970 save percentage. The Jets outshoot the Knights in every game, but Fleury steals at least two or three games. That's what you need in the play-offs: your goalie stealing games for you. I got some heat when I said Tuukka Rask was the reason the Bruins lost to Tampa. Rask didn't play badly, but he didn't steal them a game. In the last two games of that series, which Boston lost, the Bruins outshot Tampa Bay 60–49 and were outscored 7–4, and you're not going to win a series when that happens.

Ron and I are in Winnipeg for Game 5 and Vegas wins 2–1 to win the series. Fleury breaks the Jets' hearts, making 31 saves to win the game. Fleury has stolen the series for Vegas. It's the best goaltending performance I've seen in a series. I think if the Jets could've got by Vegas, they would've gone on to win the Cup.

* * *

The next morning, we get up early and head out to Regina for the Memorial Cup game between the Hamilton Bulldogs and the Swift Current Broncos. It's the 100th Memorial Cup tournament. We land at the Regina air-port, and there are three or four women at the airport holding a sign: WELCOME TO REGINA, RON AND DON. Makes you feel good when you see something like that, and Ron and I take a bunch of pictures with the ladies.

Before the game, I watch the Hamilton and Swift Current players get off the bus and head into the rink. They look just like NHLers—all dressed up sharp and with good-looking haircuts, except for one thing: nobody's holding a cup of coffee. Almost every NHL player has a coffee in his hand when he arrives at the rink. They need it to wake up from their naps.

We wait for the game to start sitting in the office of John Paddocks, the coach of the Pats.

I'm so proud to meet and be on the ice with the soldiers of the Royal Regina Rifle Regiment and Princess Patricia's Canadian Light Infantry—the Regina Pats are named after them. When we're on camera, I ask Ron to introduce the soldiers. Ron had just looked at a sheet of paper with the soldiers' names for a second, but he knew all their names and ranks.

Ron really is amazing at things like that. Years ago, he used to do updates during the games on *Hockey Night in Canada*. We'd be watching the Leafs game and he'd be eating a cookie or talking with somebody, and then he'd suddenly say, "Excuse me," go on the air and rattle off the name of the player who scored the goal—even add a little something about the guy—and then he'd go back to his cookie or his conversation, never missing a beat. When we're doing "Coach's Corner," I'll sometimes ask out of the blue where a player is from or who he played junior for, and Ron will know. Don't ask me how he does it; it's not a set-up.

Ron really is unbelievable. Occasionally, before *Hockey Night in Canada* goes to air, Ron and I are asked to do a promo or a video for the police or military. I'll get the script and struggle through it, whereas Ron takes a quick glance and does a fantastic job. I think this is the first time I have praised him in any of my books. He is the best. I hope he doesn't get a big head.

The game ends and Hamilton beats Swift Current 2–1 in a great game. MacKenzie Entwistle of the Bulldogs scores the game's first goal. I remember watching him play for the Toronto Marlies minor midgets. I really liked him back then, and he's had a good junior career. He was drafted by the Arizona Coyotes and was traded to the Hawks this summer. I get a kick out of seeing kids I watched when they were 15 making it to the NHL.

* * *

After the game, we head home and get right back on the road for the final. Who would have believed Washington and Las Vegas would be playing for the Cup?

We're in Las Vegas for Game 1. At ice level, you can't hear yourself think. The crowd is going nuts and guys with swords are fighting on the ice. I guess it's good for hockey. As Ron and I are waiting to go on the ice, I see a guy with a great jacket with different Golden Knights logos on it. So I ask him if I can borrow it for the opening. Looking back on it later, I guess everybody thought I was rooting for Vegas, which I kinda was.

After the opening, I thank him and ask who he is. His name is George Salami. Ron asks me what his name is, and when I answer, "George Salami," Ron thinks I've screwed up another name. After the first period, we're waiting to go on "Coach's Corner" and we look down, and guess who we see working on the ice. It's George Salami. We see him the next day at the morning skate, and he tells us he's from Windsor, Ontario, and he is the chief of the ice crew at the T-Mobile Arena in Vegas. Boy, was it hot in Vegas for the series, but the ice was in good shape, thanks to George.

The Knights win the first game and they look pretty good, and I think they have a good chance to go on and win the Cup. The next day, I see four or five of the Vegas players on television, talking about being the Golden Misfits and no one believing in them. I get that bad feeling again. Up to now, the Knights have had that little "us against the world" thing going in the dressing room, but now it's gone. They're turning into celebrities. The Capitals are keeping their mouths shut, and when they do say something, they're saying the right things. I see Ron and tell him I think Washington is going to win.

After the first period of Game 2, we're getting ready to do "Coach's Corner." I cannot have anybody in the studio — no cameraman, no floor manager — and it needs to be dark. If I see anybody, it throws me off. It's funny that I can do an opening in front of 18,000 screaming fans, but I need a dark, empty set for "Coach's Corner." At the T-Mobile Arena, we're shooting in a suite in the middle of the crowd, which is hard for me. I can hardly hear Ron with the crowd yelling and the music blaring. Our producer, Kathy Broderick, tells everybody to get out of the suite.

In the last two minutes, I start talking about how Quebec City should get a team. Ron gets me good. I don't want to mention that the owner of the Boston Bruins, Jeremy Jacobs, has said Quebec shouldn't get a team. But Ron mentions Jacobs. I'm a little mad at him, and as I am talking, I look up and see the commissioner of the NHL, Gary Bettman. I'm a little taken back. He just came up to say hello, but Ron invites him on, and when those two go on the air together, you never know what's going to happen. I tell Gary that Quebec has the rink, the money, strong ownership and most important, they've kept their mouth shut and they deserve to get a team. After the segment, Kathy takes a picture of Ron, Gary and me on the set. When Gary leaves, Kathy says, "Sorry, Don. I can kick everybody out, but not Commissioner Bettman." Kathy is no dummy.

Vegas loses. Fleury is a shell of the goalie he was in the Winnipeg series. If he doesn't start playing better, Vegas is done. The Knights outshoot Washington 39–26 and lose. The score is 3–2 late in the third, and Caps goalie Braden Holtby robs Alex Tuch with the save of the playoffs. You never know; if the Knights had scored on that shot and tied it up, it could have been a different series.

* * *

The next morning, we fly out to Washington for Game 3, which the Capitals win. First game back home is always a gimme game.

The next day, Ron and I go to the morning skate. The top prospects for NHL drafts are there—every year, Ron and I do a segment where we introduce them. I'm not in the mood to do the segment this year. There are only a few Canadians, and I'm not sure the idea isn't getting a little old. I see the kids, and I'm not sure *they* even want to do it. But Ron and Kathy talk me into it. So we do it, off the cuff, with only one camera and no makeup.

I remember the first time we did this segment. It was in Montreal, and there were going to be five players making the rounds. Three of them were English and two were French. The two French players were going to be introduced at centre ice at the Forum, and I was going to have the three English players on "Coach's Corner." The next day, one of the papers said I was a racist because I didn't have the French players on. Same old stuff.

There is Noah Dobson (he'll go 12th overall to the New York Islanders), Brady Tkachuk (fourth overall to Ottawa), Rasmus Dahlin (first overall to Buffalo), Andrei Svechnikov (second overall to Carolina), Quinn Hughes (seventh overall to Vancouver), Evan Bouchard (10th overall to Edmonton) and Filip Zadina (sixth overall to Detroit), and they all look sharp in their new suits and fresh haircuts. I tell them to say their names, where they played and who their favorite player is and why. Someone asks, "Do I have to say why I like that player?" I tell them to keep it short and just say who they like. You can see that they're all nervous. Things go well and we show it on "Coach's Corner" that night.

After the shoot, Dahlin comes up and asks for a photo, which kind of surprises me. Later, I'll read that the media asked him what the highlight of his first NHL game was; he said it was meeting Don Cherry. His father was a big fan and had all my Rock'em Sock'em DVDs. Luke Fox wrote about it on *Sportsnet* the next day:

*Admittedly starstruck, Rasmus Dahlin says the highlight of
his first NHL game as a spectator—Game 4 of the Stanley
Cup Final in Washington—wasn't so much talking a little
hockey with Nicklas Bäckström or William Karlsson.*

It was meeting Don Cherry.

*The Swedish phenom has been watching Cherry's vid-
eos since age five because his dad was a fan.*

*"Oh, yeah, that was awesome. He had a sick suit,"
Dahlin said. "I just wanted to take a picture. He said to
me, 'Thumbs up,' so I did thumbs up."*

Then someone tells me that one of the players was at the
NHL combine and called his agent to make sure he had a
new suit and shoes, because he was going to be on "Coach's
Corner." I realize I've got to smarten up and realize that this
is a big deal for these players.

* * *

After Ron and I do the Game 4 opening on the ice, I go to
a little room by myself and watch the game. Ron goes
upstairs to the suite with the rest of the *Hockey Night in
Canada* crew. I can't have people around me, talking,
while I'm watching the game. It's the same when Tim and
I scout the minor midgets. I see scouts talking away while
the game is on. Tim and I hardly say a word when we're
concentrating on the game.

With a couple of minutes left in the first period, I head
up to the suite to meet Ron. As I'm going through the
crowd, I'm posing for picture after picture. Some guy

who's half-drunk is screaming, "Why do you hate the Caps?" I push my way through and try to ignore him. The more I ignore him, the madder he gets. Just as I'm about to enter the suite, he comes over and punches me in the stomach. Not hard, but hard enough.

It reminds me of what a security guard at the Air Canada Centre told me a few years ago. I was introducing a soldier during a Leafs game, and as I made my way back to the studio, a ton of people were pushing and shoving and taking my picture. It was a madhouse. When I reached a hallway, this big security guard pulled me aside and said, "Grapes, I know you like being close to the crowd, and they are all good people. But it just takes one jerk. If some guy that didn't like you had a knife, he could stab you and melt back into the crowd and we'd never find him. You got to be careful."

Maybe I've got to be smarter.

This "Coach's Corner" is a special one. The Knights have played great but are down 3–0 after the first period. I criticize Fleury, which Ron doesn't like. Then we have a special guest: four-star general and chief of staff of the US Army, Mark A. Milley. General Milley has just come from a Gold Star family event with President Donald Trump. A Gold Star family is one that has lost a son, daughter, mother or father in combat. The honour started in World War I, when President Woodrow Wilson didn't want widows and mothers dressed in black, mourning, if a loved one was killed. So they decided to give them an armband or badge that had a gold star, signifying their family member's sacrifice.

Milley's grandparents were born in St. John's, Newfoundland. They moved down to Boston, and the general was born in Winchester, Massachusetts, where he and his father became Bruins fans. He tells a funny story about his father, who lived in Somerville, Massachusetts, and served in the 4th Marine Division of the US Marine Corps in World War II—the first unit to land on the beaches at Iwo Jima. His father didn't know much about the South Pacific, the general says, and he thought there'd be some ice that he could play hockey on, so he brought his hockey skates with him!

On tonight's broadcast, we're commemorating the Battle of Normandy, and General Milley knows all about the Canadians and Juno Beach. When I was in Afghanistan, the Canadian commander told me that if our troops needed anything like helicopters or supplies, General Milley was the guy to ask. He played hockey for Princeton and was the captain of the team. And, like I said, he's a lifetime Bruins fan. Ron asks him to name his favourite player, and he answers Bobby Orr. What a guy!

I think it was one of the best "Coach's Corners."

By the end of the second period, Washington has scored four goals on 15 shots, and they end up with six goals on 23 shots. At the other end, Holtby plays spectacularly. The Caps win and we are heading back to Vegas.

Fleury is really struggling. His save percentage for the series is under .900, and you're never going to win the Stanley Cup with your goalie playing like that. I bet the Jets are at home, saying, "Why couldn't he have played like that against us?"

* * *

There's an extra day off before Game 5 in Vegas. After the morning skate, we head off to the Luxor Hotel and see the *Titanic* exhibit, and it's fantastic. I usually don't do things like this, but if you are ever in Las Vegas, you have to see the *Titanic*.

There's a great bar at the Luxor Hotel, and as we are leaving Ron and I stop off for a cool one. We order two beers. I spill mine and it goes all over the floor. No one sees it but I can't let that happen, so I go to the bartender and ask for a towel. When he asks why I want a towel, I tell him I spilled a beer on the floor. He tells me to never mind, he'll get it. It's hard to believe but the bartender comes over with another beer for us. It's nice and cold.

If the Caps win tonight, we won't have to go back to Washington. At the morning skate, some of the parents and friends of the players come up and want to take a picture with me. And now I have to say another thing about Ron: he doesn't have a jealous bone in his body. He's glad they want a picture taken only with me. When we're walking through airports and people say, "Great show, Don," it doesn't seem to bother him either. Maybe one day, he'll tell me it does. And the funny thing is, Ron never, ever takes a bad picture.

I don't know why, but I love morning skates. It was even true when I coached. Kathy brings Ron and me coffee and muffins. She doesn't have to do that, but she's one of us and is just that type of person.

A TV reporter named Erin interviews me for television

in Washington. She says she's from Canada and asks me who's going to win tonight. I say, "Washington will win the Cup tonight."

"How can you be so sure?"

"Because I am the expert, and that's why you have me on."

She doesn't know what to say to that.

During the game, it looks like a player high-sticks an opponent. The ref who's four feet away doesn't call it, but the other ref calls the penalty from 50 feet away. I go on "Coach's Corner" and say, "How can the ref who's right there not call, but the guy at the blue line calls it?" I don't want to mention the ref's name and embarrass him, but Ron mentions his name. Of course, I can just imagine what might happen: Somebody might go up to that ref and say, "Cherry criticized you tonight."

It wasn't a high stick, but it looked like one. When the replay is slowed down, you can see the player was hit by his own stick. I think when something like that happens, the refs need help. I think they should have a guy in the rink who can call down to the refs and say, "It wasn't a high stick." Get the call right and help get the ref off the hook.

The Capitals do go on to win, and Ovechkin wins the Conn Smythe Trophy as playoff MVP. If you ask me, Holtby should've won it. If you switch goalies, Vegas wins in a sweep.

After the final game, Ron and I have a few beers, nothing spectacular. I tell him he can go out with the rest of the guys, but I guess he wants to be all right for the flight home. So it's our usual routine when we're on the road. After the game, we head back to the hotel. I take a shower and get my TV makeup off. I get into my T-shirt and sweat pants and head over to Ron's room. Ron always has the door ajar. Between two chairs, he puts the table, with a towel spread out over it. There's peanuts and popcorn (which is Ron's specialty), and of course, there are 12 Bud Lights on ice. Ron's room is always nice and neat.

I've got an early flight out of Vegas, and for some reason, Ron's flying out later in the afternoon. He has to fly through Minnesota to get to Toronto, if you can believe it. I still don't know why we couldn't get a direct flight to Toronto.

In the morning, I walk by his door, and I know he's asleep. He likes to sleep in when he can. Ron's a great sleeper, even on planes. One time, we got on the plane and Ron fell asleep right away. The plane sat at the gate for about an hour for some reason. I convinced everybody in first class to start to get up, as if the plane had landed. So everybody was getting up out of their seats, and I shook Ron awake, saying, "Come on, let's go." Ron got up, half-asleep, and lined up to get off the plane. Everybody had a good laugh.

As I pass by his door, I put a note under it. It reads, "A good time was had by all." Which I always say at the end of our sessions.

It's 8 a.m., and I meet Kathy in the lobby. We're getting ready to head out to the airport, and who comes down to say goodbye? Ron. I guess after two months on the road, he feels he had to say goodbye. I'm touched. I won't see Ron until the start of next season.

Kathy and I start our marathon trip back home to Toronto. We have to change planes in Atlanta. We land in Terminal A and have to walk all the way to Terminal E. If you've ever been to the Atlanta airport, you know how far a walk that is. We land in Toronto and have to walk miles to get to customs. When we get there, talk about chaos. One guy is yelling, in broken English and with a mean tone, "Keep moving, keep moving." There's got to be 100 people in line, snaking through the customs area. People are like zombies, pushing and shoving. They have those machines where you scan your passport, and a lot of people don't know how to use them. I have to say, Toronto is one of the worst airports to land in.

We finally make it through, and Kathy and I say goodbye. I won't see her till the start of next season. I can't tell you how much she helps Ron and me on the road.

I finally get home, and Luba and the dogs—Jake, Billy and Buddy—are asleep. I have a cold one and go to bed. It's been 12 hours since we left Vegas.

I'll close it off here with one of Ron's puns. A few years ago, Ron and I were walking, and I wondered what those dark spots on the sidewalk were. Ron told me it was people spitting their gum on the ground. I still cannot believe people would do that. During this year's finals, we were in Washington before Game 3, walking to the rink. I pointed to all the spots on the ground and say to Ron, "Someone should clean that up." Ron snapped back, "No, they'd probably just gum it up."

FINAL THOUGHTS

I am glad that a good guy like Barry Trotz, from Winnipeg, got to win a Stanley Cup. Barry paid his dues, first coaching the Dauphin Kings in the Winnipeg Junior Hockey League, and then seven years in the AHL, winning the Calder Cup in 1994 with the Portland Pirates before heading to the NHL with Nashville. He coached 20 years in the NHL before he won the Cup.

It's ironic, but as I am writing this, I'm hearing the news that Barry is leaving Washington and is now a "free agent." This season was the last on Barry's four-year contract, but there was a clause that said if he won the Stanley Cup, he got a two- or three-year extension with a bump in salary. He was not happy with the money Washington was offering, so he left. Barry's situation is like mine in Boston was, or Scotty Bowman's in Montreal—we were both offered contracts, but turned them down because it was time to go. Both Barry and Scotty left after winning the Cup.

And I've just heard that Barry signed with the Islanders for five years at $4 million a year. Good for him.

You've got to have a little luck to win the Cup. Remember the first round of the playoffs against Columbus? The Blue Jackets with the first game 4–3 in overtime. In Game 2, the Caps poured 58 shots on Blue Jackets goalie Sergei Bobrovsky and lost in overtime. The Blue Jackets stole the first two games and it looked like curtains for Washington as the teams went back to Columbus. Game 3 went into double overtime, the Blue Jackets rang two off the post, and the Caps scored as the puck went off a Blue Jackets defenceman and into the net for the winner. If the Blue Jackets had won that game, there was no way Washington was coming back. The Capitals won the next three games and moved on. So, a little bit of luck changed the Capitals' fate.

Something else happened in Game 2 of that series that helped the Capitals win the Cup. At the start of the playoffs, Barry Trotz went with Philipp Grubauer in net. Braden Holtby sat on the bench. In Game 2, Trotz pulled Grubauer after the second period, after the Blue Jackets scored four goals on 22 shots. Holtby went in, and even though the Caps lost in overtime, Holtby started the next game and reeled off four straight wins. Like I said earlier in the book, nothing can motivate a player like being embarrassed. Holtby won't admit it, but he was embarrassed at not starting in the playoffs, and he wanted to prove he was the guy who could win a Stanley Cup. One thing that might have helped Braden this year was that he only played 54 games in the regular. He played well over 60 games in each of the three years before. I think he was better rested this year than any other year.

Another guy who was a big factor, though you might not think about him, was Brooks Orpik. He's six foot three and 220 pounds. He battled all the tough guys in the corners, as well as in front of the net, and made sure Holtby could see the puck. He doesn't hit a lot, but when he does, he hits to hurt. He gets the puck out of trouble by chipping it off the glass or flipping it to centre ice. Bet you didn't know he led the NHL in these playoffs with a plus-17 in 24 games. He played about 17 minutes a game and even had a game-winning goal.

It's funny: Everybody says the league is moving to smaller, faster defencemen who can rush with the puck, and the biggest plus player in the Stanley Cup playoffs was a big, stay-at-home defenceman who's an 11-year veteran of the league. I read yesterday that the Caps traded him to Denver, and they are going to put him on waivers and then buy him out of his contract, which pays over $5 million a year. A team with a young defence should pick him up. He's 37, but as they say, you're only as good as your last shift, and his was pretty good. He could help a team like the Leafs by teaching their young defencemen how it's done.

* * *

I am at home, recovering from the trip back from Vegas, and I read that Max Domi has been traded to Montreal for Alex Galchenyuk. Montreal is tough, maybe the toughest place to play, so I hope Max gets off to a good start. I've known him since he was seven years old, when he played minor hockey with my grandson Del. Later, I watched him when he played for the Don Mills Flyers in the Greater Toronto Hockey League.

I know that it may seem hard to believe, but I do pull for Montreal to do well. Now more than ever, with Max there. Maybe it's because Kirk Muller is assistant coach there, or because they're a Canadian team from the Original Six, but I'd like to see them make the 2019 play-offs. I hope Carey Price plays like only he can play and can steal them some games. If that happens, I think they'll battle for a playoff spot.

Montreal's GM, Marc Bergevin, drafted Jesperi Kotkaniemi from Finland instead of Brady Tkachuk. Brady's a big kid who looks like he's ready to play in the NHL right now. He's a big power forward with great bloodlines. Brady's father, Keith, was a great NHLer, and Brady plays with his father's edge and hits a ton. Even in the *Montreal Gazette*, they were talking about how they thought Tkachuk was going to be Montreal's pick. When Montreal announced they were taking Kotkaniemi, the TV cameras showed two older Canadiens fans, all dressed up in their Montreal sweaters. You should've seen the look of shock on their faces. They looked at each other and said, "Who?" I hope for Marc's sake that it all works out, because the fans are restless in Montreal.

The Leafs took Riley Stotts of the Calgary Hitmen in the third round. When Riley was playing at the Under-17 Challenge, he had his skates off in the dressing room and someone stepped back and badly cut a couple of his toes. He's okay now. It reminded me of when I was in Vancouver and we won the Western Hockey League championship in 1969. We were in the dressing room, celebrating, and the trainer was yelling at everybody to take their skates off. One of the Vancouver players was being interviewed, and he came into the dressing room with his skates on and stepped on someone's foot. There was blood everywhere. I felt bad for the guy whose foot was cut, but I'm sorry to say it didn't slow down the celebration one bit.

* * *

I'm sitting at Wolfe Island, having a cold one while watching the NHL Awards. Connor McDavid wins the Ted Lindsay Award, which is for the best player in the NHL, and what makes it even more special is that players vote on it, not the media. It's hard to believe Connor scored 108 points last year on a team that didn't even make the playoffs. They got it right; he is the best player on the NHL. Sidney Crosby's a close second.

Then Taylor Hall, from Kingston, Ontario, wins the Hart Trophy. The Hart Trophy is for the player who is "most valuable to his team." Taylor deserves it. He had a 25-point scoring streak and ended up with 39 goals and 93 points, helping the New Jersey Devils get into the playoffs for the first time in six years.

I remember watching these two when they were just kids. I first saw Connor when he was 15 years old, playing against 16-year-olds. He scored a goal and two assists in a 3–2 win. I remember walking out of the rink and telling Tim, "We'd better keep our eye on the McDavid kid." Then we watched him when he played for the Marlies in his minor midget year.

I remember watching Taylor, who was playing for Kingston, in the OHL Minor Midget Cup. I was watching Kingston play early in the morning, and they asked me to pick the best player at the end of the game. I picked Taylor, who hadn't scored a goal. They came to me and said, "He didn't score a goal. How can he be the best player?" I said, "You said to pick the best player, and he's the best player on the ice, even though he didn't score." I think Taylor was a little embarrassed. He played later that day and scored six goals.

2018 PLAYOFFS AND BEYOND

Wouldn't it be great to see Connor and Taylor on the same line? Taylor is just what Connor needs: someone who can skate with him, is as fast as him and is a trigger man, so he could take some scoring pressure off McDavid. Someone who is a friend of his and has been his roommate. Most important, he wanted to play in Edmonton. Now throw Leon Draisaitl on the other side. It would be one of the best lines in hockey. Hard to believe the Edmonton Oilers traded Hall for an okay defenceman. I remember seeing the Oilers coach yelling at Taylor and making him go and sit at the end of the bench. I knew that was it for Taylor in Edmonton. I look back at standing in a freezing cold rink at 9:30 p.m. at night watching Connor and Taylor starting their journey to the NHL and now here they are winning the Hart and Ted Lindsay trophies.

* * *

It's July 1, the first day of free agency, and John Tavares is now in the Toronto Maple Leafs fold.

I remember when Mike Babcock signed on as coach of the Leafs back in 2015. In his first interview in Toronto, the interviewer said, "You know, Mike, free agents will never come to Toronto for any money." Mike, full of confidence and a little bit of arrogance—which I like—answered, "That may have been in the past, but we will get things rolling and the free agents will come here." Tavares just proved Mike's point.

Yes, I know Tavares is making a lot of dough here, but think of the taxes in Toronto as compared with Las Vegas,

San Jose or anywhere else in the States. John will now be living in a fishbowl, and will be feeling the pressure of being captain. He will have the pressure of dealing with the Toronto media. Every time the Leafs lose, John will be front and centre, answering the questions from the media.

And Auston Matthews has just had a mountain lifted off his back. He won't have to be the front-and-centre guy after every game.

I have watched John since he was 14 years old, playing with the Toronto Marlies minor midgets. He was great back then. You could tell he was going to be a superstar. In fact, he was the first player to be given special status by the Ontario Hockey League, allowing him to be drafted a few months before he turned 15. The Oshawa Generals took him first overall. Only two players were younger than John when they started playing junior hockey at the top level in Ontario: Denis Potvin, with the Ottawa 67's, and Bobby Orr—he was 14, and he played for the Generals too.

I coached against John when he played for Team Orr in the Canadian Hockey League Top Prospects game. He was the best player on the ice until he hurt his shoulder after someone on my team hit him behind the net. After the game, someone from the media actually asked me if I'd sent someone out to hurt him. Sometimes, the questions some of the media ask just make me shake my head.

I knew Tavares was on his way to Toronto when the Leafs let James van Riemsdyk—and his 36 goals in 2017–18—walk away so easily. I knew the Leafs had to get those goals back from somewhere. With van Riemsdyk gone, they made some salary cap room for John, but wait till all their young stars' contracts come up. That's when Toronto's new GM, Kyle Dubas, will earn his salary.

I think Lou Lamoriello, the new GM of the Islanders, made a good move in signing Barry Trotz, who just won the Cup as coach of the Capitals, to coach the Islanders. But really, who wants to play on the Island? Their new rink won't be ready for years. In the meantime, they're playing some games in Brooklyn and some in Nassau Coliseum. The Islanders could've offered Tavares one more year, but he made the right decision. Seeing that picture of Tavares when he was a kid, sleeping in Leafs pyjamas, with a Leafs pillow and bedspread, you know where his heart is.

Imagine: seven years, $77 million. It makes you wonder how much Bobby Orr would make today. John had 37 goals and 47 assists last year and was a minus-12. In 1974–75, Bobby had 46 goals and 89 assists and was plus-80—not even his best year, as he was plus-124 one time. He received 101 minutes in penalties, got into three fights, and he blocked shots and hit a ton. I know it's not fair to compare John with the best player who ever played the game, but if John is making that kind of money, then for a player like Bobby, I think you'd have to start out by giving him part ownership of the team and then go from there.

* * *

Looking back at this year, one event stands out as the highlight. I got a call a few months into the season from Karen, who's with the Boston Bruins Alumni. She wanted to know if I would attend a 40-year reunion of the '77–78 team that set an NHL record by having 11 players who scored at least 20 goals. They wanted to fly in the players and me (of course I was the coach) and have a dinner and drop the puck at centre ice at a Bruins game.

At first, I didn't want to go. I never seem to have a good experience at this kind of thing. The last reunion I went to was back in the mid-'90s, for the 1953 Barrie Flyers winning the Memorial Cup. I'd said I'd go, so Rose and I drove up to Barrie and arrived at Molson Park. They had a beautiful room set up with all kinds of food and drink. We were there for a few minutes and I started to get some bad vibes. Not a friendly feeling. It was like, "Oh, here's the big shot on *Hockey Night in Canada*." I don't know if that was true or not, but that was the vibe I was getting. I told Rose, "Come on, let's go."

Rose said, "We just checked in a half hour ago and now you want to leave?" But we left.

So, I was going to say no to the Bruins reunion, but then I thought, "What if everybody goes and I don't show up?" I hadn't seen some of those guys for 40 years, and we did have a good time that season. Just think about it: to have that many 20-goal scorers, you have three lines with each player scoring 20 or more, then you've got someone on the fourth line with 20 goals and a defenceman with 20. That's why I never matched lines. I could throw out any line and they would be able to score or check. The only exception was that when Guy Lafleur was on the ice, I put on Don Marcotte.

I found out the get-together was Rick Middleton's idea. Here's a quick story about Rick. It was late in the season,

and Rick needed one more goal for a big bonus. I was dou-
ble-shifting him, trying to get him that goal. The Bruins'
GM, Harry Sinden, was not too happy about the whole situation. I told the rest of the guys that when Ricky scored to
earn his bonus, they should play it cool and not get Harry
mad. With a few games left in the season, Ricky scored—
and the whole team jumped on the ice to congratulate him.

I knew that Harry would be steaming. So after the game,
I again told the guys to cool it. Now, earlier in the book, I
told you that one of Ricky's nicknames was Eddie, because
he looked like Eddie Munster. When Harry walked into
the dressing room, the whole team started to chant,
"Eddie! Eddie! Eddie!" Again, Harry did not seem pleased.
I believe Harry was happy for Ricky, but as a general
manager, he could not appear to be overjoyed at the
thought of a coach working with a player to take bonus
money from the team.

The reunion was February 13. The Bruins were playing
the Calgary Flames that night. I decided to go, but I had
to fly in that day. The players—Peter McNab, who scored
41 goals; Terry O'Reilly, 29; Bobby Schmautz and Stan
Jonathan, 27 each; Jean Ratelle and Rick Middleton, 25
each; Gregg Sheppard, 23; Brad Park, 22; and Don
Marcotte and Bobby Miller, 20 (Wayne Cashman, who
scored 24 goals, couldn't make it)—flew in the night
before and had a great dinner. The next day, they met for
breakfast and then headed over to the TD Garden to meet
the current Bruins players. I talked to the guys afterward
and they said the current players were really into talking
to the guys and didn't just brush them off. I met Rick

Middleton at the hotel, and around two o'clock, the guys and I signed a ton of posters and pictures before getting on a bus and heading off to the rink.

I thought it was just going to be a simple ceremony, where we'd march onto the ice and drop the puck. It was so much more. When we got to the arena, everybody did interviews with the media. All around the rink, they displayed the players' pictures and the number of goals they'd scored. They had video highlights of the goals on the big screen and they were giving out terrific posters of the players. The Bruins organization really did it up royally.

Afterwards, I did an interview with Andy Brickley, who played for the Bruins in the '90s and is now one of their broadcasters. I went down a hallway, and who should I run into but the Calgary Flames' GM, Brian Burke. Now, a lot of you know that Brian and I were not great friends; in fact, we had a feud going when he was the GM in Toronto. It all started when the Leafs asked me (I assume without Brian's knowledge) to go over to the Air Canada Centre and introduce some soldiers in the crowd. The Rangers were playing the Leafs, and their coach, John Tortorella, and players were clapping. I noticed that Leafs coach Ron Wilson was not clapping. Now, I didn't like Ron and he didn't like me for various reasons, and this was the straw that broke the camel's back. When I got back to the studio, I blasted Ron Wilson.

Brian took offence. In fact, he said, "There is a certain guy on TV that has been unfair to the Leafs. I don't want to take anything away from the playoffs. I will deal with the situation when the playoffs are over." I went on TV and said, "Oh, Brian Burke is out to get me. I'm shaking in my boots." It went downhill from there.

The sad thing about it is that Brian and I were friends before all this started. He would send me St. Patrick's Day cards and books on Lord Admiral Horatio Nelson, the hero of Trafalgar. Brian had done a thesis on Nelson when he was in university, where he was a teammate of Ron Wilson's.

Tonight, as we met, we shook hands. Life's too short.

Since leaving the Flames in April, Brian has been working for Rogers Sportsnet on the hockey broadcasts, and he does a great job. He has done just about every job in hockey, so he does have good insights into the game. But I have to admit, I like him better with his tie done up.

Before the game, we were in the tunnel, ready to go onto the ice. All the players had their sweaters on. And I had a déjà vu moment. For an instant, I got the feeling we were about to play a game.

They ran a great video on the big screen about all the players. Then they introduced us one at a time. We got a great roar from the crowd and both the Bruins and Flames players were banging their sticks on the boards. I think Terry O'Reilly got the biggest cheer. I was the last one introduced. We lined up to drop the puck and the Flames' Mark Giordano and the Bruins' Zdeno Chára came to centre ice. Chára looked like he was seven foot five on skates. We got a great picture of everybody, and we got another big cheer from the crowd when we left. It was great to know that the Bruins organization and the fans still appreciated what we did 40 years ago.

All of us looked like we were in good shape, but Peter McNab looked like a movie star. He looked younger than when he played. I laughed when an interviewer asked him what hockey was like 40 years ago. He said, "Oh, it was big boy hockey." Even though we had the toughest team in hockey, Peter wasn't a fighter. I can only remember him getting into one fight. He was our 40-goal scorer and I didn't want him to fight.

Peter told the story of the only time I pulled him off the ice. It was Game 3 of the '78 final against Montreal. The game was in Boston Garden, so I had the last line change. For some reason, Scotty Bowman put on all his tough guys. I had a line of Peter McNab at centre, with Terry O'Reilly and John Wensink on the wings, so I had two tough guys with Peter. When I saw that Scotty had put on Pierre Bouchard and Gilles Lupien, I took off Peter and put on Stan Jonathan. Peter told me that was the happiest moment of his life. Stan and Pierre got into one of the best fights in hockey history; there was blood all over the ice. Lupien and Wensink went at it as well, and linesman John D'Amico got cut and was covered in blood. Yep, Peter, it was big boy hockey back then.

Rick Middleton and Cam Neely did a great job of putting things together. Everybody went way above the call of duty. The current players and the fans were so gracious and seemed to appreciate what we did. After leaving the team, I would watch the Bruins on TV, but I never felt like I was part of the team or the organization. But the way everybody treated us on this occasion made us feel like we were still really part of the Bruins.

It's hard to put this thought into words, but for me, that event was the final chapter of my relationship with the Boston Bruins. I had been with the club since I was 15 years old, and this was the way to close the book on it.

* * *

The end of the playoffs means another hockey season is over. The playoffs are, and have always been, the most exciting and the most fun for me, as a player, and then as a coach, and finally as a broadcaster. Don't get me wrong; the playoffs is a tough row to hoe for players, coaches and yes, even broadcasters. Ron and I are on every other night (actually, for the first half, Ron is on *every* night) for two months. And we've been doing this a long time.

I have to admit that I sometimes say to myself, "Where has the time gone?" It seems like yesterday that Ron was hired to be the host of *Hockey Night in Canada*. He was a little twerp when he first came aboard, but I have to admit I would not be doing "Coach's Corner" without him.

Yes, it true there are more days behind me than ahead of me, and who knows how long Rogers will put up with me. I still get butterflies the day of "Coach's Corner," just like I did when I played and coached; I love that feeling.

I've also loved working on this book with Tim; it's a labour of love. Tim lives across the street, so I would go over there early in the morning with a coffee and we'd discuss what happened the night before in hockey, the world, and of course, the book. As we'd sit on the porch with the sun coming up, I'd sip the coffee and think about how lucky I am, and I'd say to myself, "Thank you, Lord."

I hope you have enjoyed reading the book as much as Timothy and I enjoyed writing it. I really have to thank Scott, Brad, Kristin and all my players at Penguin Random House Canada for letting us do our thing, as they say. The book was a joy to write. I know it's not a book for a rocket scientist, but a lot of people seem to like it, and I hope you did too.

A good time was had by all.

All the best to you and your family.

Don Cherry

INDEX

PHOTO CREDITS AND PERMISSIONS

Insert 2

Page i (bottom) © Heinz Kluetmeier/*Sports Illustrated*/Getty Images

Page ii (top) © Rusty Kennedy/AP file

Page iii © Steve Babineau/NHLI/Getty Images

Page iv (top) © CP Picture Archive/The Canadian Press

Page v © Paul Szep/*The Boston Globe*/Getty Images

Page vi. Reprinted with the kind permission of the Toronto Maple Leafs.

Page vii (bottom) © Chris O'Meara/AP Photo

Page viii (top) © Brian Babineau/NHLI/Getty Images; (bottom) © Kathy Broderick

Interior

Page 130 © Bruce Bennett Studios/Getty Images

Page 201 © Portnoy/Hockey Hall of Fame

TEXT PERMISSIONS

Page 46. The *Winnipeg Free Press* excerpt, dated September 7, 1972, is reprinted with the kind permission of the *Winnipeg Free Press*.

Page 269. The *Sportsnet* excerpt, from "Quick Shifts: 8 Thoughts on the Toronto Marlies Magic" by Luke Fox (dated June 15, 2018), is reprinted with the kind permission of *Sportsnet*.

Most fans of DON CHERRY know him for his blistering seven minutes of "Coach's Corner" on *Hockey Night in Canada*, but they might have forgotten Don's incredible journey through the world of hockey. In 1955, he played his one and only NHL game for the Boston Bruins. He then went on to coach in just about every level of hockey, from high school to the American League to the NHL to International to the OHL. Don won a state High School Championship, a Canada Cup, Coach of the Year in the AHL and the NHL, and has a .601 winning percentage in the NHL. After his coaching career, a chance appearance on *Hockey Night in Canada* launched a 35-yearlong broadcasting career. In 2004, Don was voted the 7th All-Time Greatest Canadian and in 2015, Don and his "Coach's Corner" partner, Ron MacLean, were inducted into Canada's Walk of Fame. His Rock'em Sock'em videos are all-time bestsellers and his syndicated radio show, *Grapeline*, has been on the air for over 30 years. Don's just about done it all: player, coach, television and radio star, restaurateur and bestselling author.

ALSO AVAILABLE

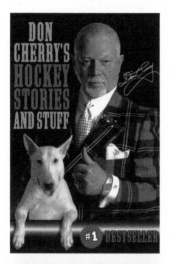

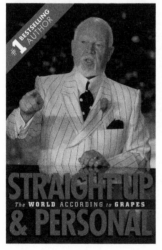

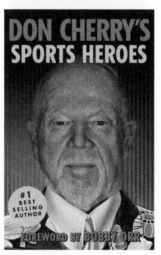